PATHWAY TO Recovery

A Spiritually Based Program of Recovery

JOHN MARTIN

WESTBOW
PRESS®
A DIVISION OF THOMAS NELSON
& ZONDERVAN

WestBow Press books may be ordered through booksellers or by contacting:

WestBow Press
A Division of Thomas Nelson & Zondervan
1663 Liberty Drive
Bloomington, IN 47403
www.westbowpress.com
844-714-3454

ISBN: 978-1-6642-0735-6 (sc)
ISBN: 978-1-6642-0737-0 (hc)
ISBN: 978-1-6642-0736-3 (e)

Library of Congress Control Number: 2020918903

Print information available on the last page.

WestBow Press rev. date: 10/15/2020

Project Sobriety

Helping Addicts Restore Life One Day at a Time

Contents

Behold, I stand at the door and knock. If anyone hears my voice and opens the door, I will come in to him and eat with him, and he with me.

—Revelation 3:20 (ESV)

Perhaps no verse of scripture has had more impact on my life than this verse. The mental image it creates for me is so instructive. There is a door that stands between me and the Lord Jesus Christ. The door is closed, and it only has only one doorknob, on my side of the door. Jesus is standing on the outside in the bright sunshine, and I am stuck on the other side of the door, in complete darkness. When Jesus knocks, I have to fumble around and open the door. When I finally open the door, all that light comes flooding in with Jesus. When I open the door and invite Jesus in, He brings in His light to illuminate my life. That illumination never leaves me.

Jesus has given us much, but He expects us to respond. We cannot sit idly by and wait for Him to approach us. We must take that first step toward Him. Once we do, He is with us forever. How comforting is that?

This book is dedicated, first and foremost, to the Lord Jesus Christ, Who has given me power over my addiction. Next, this book is dedicated to all those family members who stood with me before, during, and after my stay in an addiction treatment center. There are too many to list. You know who you are. Finally, this book is dedicated my wife and to DWF, the one close friend I have outside of my family.. My wife and this friend unleashed on me what I now refer to as an unrelenting prayer attack. At my lowest and darkest point, despite being told by me to stop, they prayed for me unceasingly. I thought they were wasting their breath and shouldn't waste their prayer time on someone who was beyond God's ability to help. I am so grateful you ignored me and did the opposite by praying that much harder.

I am living proof that not one person is beyond being helped by God. The only person who cannot be helped is the one who chooses to decline the help being offered.

Thank you all so much. There are no words to express my gratitude.

Foreword
By David Funke

My relationship with John Martin makes no sense. There's always been something about this guy; I knew I wanted our relationship to continue.

Here's when it really got unexplainable: At the time John had both knees replaced, we were acquaintances but certainly not close friends. While I was driving to the hospital to visit him, I remember thinking, *What in the world am I doing? I hardly ever visit family members in the hospital, much less a casual acquaintance like John.*

I now know that I was placed in John's life, and he was placed in mine. God knew we would both go through life experiences and need an authentic and committed friend who had the wisdom and horsepower to get through them together.

My dear friend John Martin is not the guy lighting up the room, slapping people on the back and telling jokes, although he is one of the funniest people I know. He can find something funny about everyday life events.

John has depth and substance. That is why I read, slowly, every word he recorded in this book. These are the words of a deep and thoughtful man, who has taken ownership of the messes he created during his intimate relationship with alcohol.

In 2014, while I was away on vacation, John went dark on me. I thought surely he was dead, because he always responded quickly to my texts and emails. I later found out that he was, in fact, almost dead.

Before alcohol nearly killed him, John and I often enjoyed a few drinks after work. It was great fun. The problem was that I thought John was a close and trusted friend, but he was actually an extraordinarily gifted liar.

I would have my two drinks, have lots of laughs, and go home. John never told me the truth during those days. He never told me that by the time I joined him, he already had four drinks, and drinking with me was nothing more than pre-gaming. He would leave me to go do his world-class drinking at another watering hole. I had no idea.

The only time John made me angry was when he lied to me. When he began his road to recovery, I remember telling him I could not be his friend if he gave himself permission to lie to me. He has not lied to me ever since that conversation. And he will not lie to you.

John's raw words are unfiltered and from the heart. Having lived through all of this with John, I can confirm that it is all true. John Martin's life story is inspiring and empowering, and I am so very grateful for the privilege of sharing life with my dear friend.

Author's Note

If you are reading this, it is because you, a close friend, or a family member is struggling with addiction. I know something about addiction. I am a recovering alcoholic. My addiction nearly cost me everything important in life. The most important things we ever build in life are relationships. You cannot see them or feel them in the sense that you can see or feel a car, but they are there. Relationships require care and attention. Unfortunately, those of us plagued with addiction end up really only working on one relationship, the one with our drug of choice.

I have learned much about the damage addiction does to a family. The people you care about most no longer trust you. Who can blame them? We shattered their trust the last time. You see, one of the things they teach us in Alcoholics Anonymous is that we must want to get better, and we can only clean our side of the street. What does this mean? It means that somewhere deep down inside, you really want to get better. You have to want to get better for yourself, first and foremost. It seems selfish, right? In a sense, it is selfish, but in a very real sense, we may never be able to rebuild our relationships without the deep desire to get better.

On the topic of wanting to get better, it may not come right away. I went to an intake center to prove to my family that they were the ones who had a problem with my drinking, not me. In less than five minutes, I learned that I would not be safe trying to give up alcohol on my own. I was so addicted to alcohol that they were afraid the withdrawal would kill me. At its very worst, addiction robs us of our ability to see our own problems. For many weeks, I was not sure I really wanted to recover. It was a ton of work. It was painful. Some of you may not believe what I am about to tell you, but it was like my car had a mind of its own. I wanted that next drink so badly.

But a funny thing happened to me during those fights, and I mean they were vicious fights. I began to want to get better. I have said it many times, but an old-timer, whose name I don't even know, caught me very early in sobriety and told me I didn't have to relapse. I could beat this the first time if I really wanted to. I left that meeting, and for the first time, I really wanted to defeat my addiction. For the first time in fifteen years, I did not want alcohol to control all my thoughts and actions.

So this is where the second part kicks in. We can only clean our side of the street. What does this mean? It means we have broken trust with people around us. They aren't going to believe we are better because we say we are better. They'll believe we are better when they see we are better. They must see us walking what we talk, consistently, over time. Gradually, they will begin to trust us again, in most cases. Unfortunately, some relationships are broken beyond repair. We are required to take responsibility for those failures, but we cannot allow them to consume us.

Satan will use these broken relationships to try and send us back to our old ways. At the end of the process, we need to be confident that we have done all we can to mend our broken fences. We must give our all to fixing ourselves so that our relationships can be repaired. But none of this will happen if we don't want to get better for ourselves first.

In this book, you will find the journey I had to take to make peace with myself. Before I could make peace with myself, I had to make peace with God. That took a lot of time. I learned that God did not hate me. I learned that He loved me and wanted better for me. He gave me the ability to get right with Him, with myself, and then with others. He alone gave me the strength I needed to pick up the pieces, forgive myself, and move on under His power.

God bless you. I hope the words God has placed in this book find a way into your heart. You are worth the fight; God says so.

Preface

I became a Christian in 1985. It was a tumultuous time in my life, and I desperately needed guidance and direction. I found what I needed in the teachings of the Bible. I devoured God's Word for many years. My knowledge grew quickly. I taught Sunday school. I was a leader in my church. And I wrote Bible studies for high school students. Life was going well, or so I thought.

Then difficulty once again entered my life. I was struggling with the demands being placed on me personally and on my time. My mind raced uncontrollably. I had so much on my mind that I could not focus on any one thing. And the racing thoughts were interrupting my sleep. Rather than go to the doctor, I decided to self-medicate. For a while, all it took was one drink in the evening, and I could actually go to sleep and stay asleep. Over time, that one drink a couple of nights per week became one drink every evening. Before long, the amount and frequency of alcohol I consumed grew.

As you can imagine, my drinking quickly spiraled, and I was drinking more than any one person should consume. Over that course of time, a not-so-funny thing happened: I began to rely on alcohol more than God for peace of mind. That peace of mind was short-lived and quickly morphed into anger at God. How could a loving God allow my life to become such a wreck? How could God give me more than I could handle without alcohol? From there, it became anger at God for all the bad things happening in the world around me. How could a loving God allow such suffering?

At the end of my drinking career, I was not just mad at God but at everyone around me as well. Over fifteen years, I went from being a godly person seeking to serve the Lord the best way he could to being a person no one wanted to be around. Alcohol took me away from everything and everyone I loved. Satan used alcohol and my addiction to drive a huge wedge between God and me. In Matthew, Jesus says that where our treasure is, there our heart will be also. I found my heart in the bottom of an empty bottle. It was the lowest and darkest time in my life. I was completely and totally alone, with nothing but my thoughts and my alcohol. That is not a fun place.

Fortunately for me, the very people I had alienated did something extraordinary: they prayed for me. They prayed for me when I did not want prayer.

Does this sound like you or someone close to you? The good news is that there's a way out. You may find that way out here, but that's only because this work will take you into the Word, God's Word. He is your only true and lasting way out of the addiction that is consuming your life. You see, I learned a very important truth once I sobered up and started living addiction free. I learned in Alcoholics Anonymous how to live a spiritual life, not a religious life.

That spiritual way of life led me back to the faith I had wandered so far from. What you find here is my journey back to a life of faith. Make no mistake: The true text of this book is God's Word; it describes how His Word speaks to your soul. This work simply points to a handful of verses that I found helpful as I began living an addiction-free life. And the best part of all, this will apply to every aspect of your life. If you get something out of this work, all I ask is that you share it with the next person looking for a way out.

May the Lord bless you on the journey you are about to take.

Why I Wrote This Book

When I sat down to write this book, I realized I am here for two reasons only. First, I began a relationship with Jesus Christ in 1985, at the age of nineteen. Second, after my life derailed and I spent time in an addiction treatment facility, I spent a lot of time in Alcoholics Anonymous. Sounds like strange companions, right? Well, they are not so dissimilar.

Alcoholics Anonymous, while it pledges no allegiance to any form of religion, does teach its members how to live a spiritual life. AA instructs all its members to find a higher power. Without this higher power, it is impossible to beat addiction. We are told that we need a power greater than ourselves. We are told to pray every morning when we get up and every evening, before we go to sleep. At the end of every meeting, we recite the Lord's Prayer. I remember the way my very first AA meeting ended. At that meeting, and every meeting after it, we recited the Lord's Prayer. I know I have said this twice. It is not a misprint. That one act, as I would discover later, was probably the turning point in my life.

When I stood at the end of the first meeting, I could barely recite the prayer. That was part because I was under the influence of some heavy medications. It was also due to how long it had been since I had said that prayer, much less said the prayer and meant it. At that very first meeting, I flashed back to my childhood. I would pray the Lord's Prayer every night before I went to bed. For many days and weeks, I wondered why I got away from that habit.

After a lot of reflection, I realized I got away from that habit because I got away from God. I was no longer seeking Him, His help, His safety, His protection, and His direction. We all need help, safety, direction, and protection. It's a fact of life. Gradually, over several weeks, which turned into months, which turned into years, I had turned my back on God. Satan is so tricky. He used life itself to gradually change my focus from a relationship with God to serving life itself. I hope you never find yourself there. However, if you do find yourself in the dark and lonely spot I found myself in, you need to know there is a way out.

In Revelation 3:20, Jesus says, "Behold, I stand at the door and knock. If anyone hears my voice and opens the door, I will come in to him and eat with him, and he with me." This verse has been with me since 1985. It is one of the most important verses in my life. Every time I think about this verse, I envision a door that is closed with only one doorknob. Jesus is standing outside the door, but there's no knob. All Jesus can do is knock. I am standing on the inside of the door. Inside that room, it is very dark; there is no light. My side of the door has the only doorknob, and I can hear Jesus knocking. It is up to me to decide to open the door or leave it closed. Once I decide to open the door, light floods in. Jesus promises to come in and share a meal with me. He will do everything for me that I cannot do for myself (and then some).

This book has become that door for me. Like the room, my life had become very dark. I had to decide to open the door to Jesus and allow Him and His light into my life. In September of 2014, I opened the door for the first time in a very long time. What you find in this book is what I discovered when I mustered the courage and opened the door.

About Me

My name is John, and I am an alcoholic. Now there are nine words I never thought would ever leave my mouth, but now they do. Those nine words come with a lot of emotion. Gratitude because I have been given another chance. Remorse because of the trouble and worry I caused my family. Concern for the future because I never want to go back to that way of life. Happiness because I have an opportunity to enjoy my family, a treasure that many like me never get.

More important than those nine words, I am a Christian, a child of God, who struggles with addiction to alcohol. I entered treatment for alcoholism in September of 2014. When I got out of treatment, I looked long and hard for a faith-based solution to my addiction problem. I only found one, a long-term program, but I wanted something that was short and to the point. I realized that the only way I could achieve long-term sobriety was to focus on short-term success. I needed to build a toolbox quickly. I needed tools to help me get through my daily challenges. So many books have been written that I did not know where to begin. Then I got back to my faith and realized that I only needed one book: the Bible. In Alcoholics Anonymous, we are taught to find and trust our higher power.

I knew God; I just needed to learn how to truly trust Him as my higher power.

Pathway to Recovery is a program that is Bible-based and God-focused. The program is easy to follow and only takes six weeks to complete. At the end of the six weeks, you will have a toolbox that you can use on your road to recovery. And the best part, you will learn skills that will apply in every aspect of your life.

Introduction

If you or a loved one are struggling with addiction, Pathway to Recovery may be for you. This is a simple, Bible-based, and God-focused program that will bring you closer to your Creator. Alcoholics Anonymous teaches that we need a higher power if we are to beat our addiction. For me, that Higher Power is the God of the Bible. He has reconciled us since before we were even born. He has provided us with the opportunity to repent and draw closer to Him. And He has given us the playbook on how to live a satisfying, fulfilling, and God-pleasing life. All we must do is follow His plan.

In 2014, I was looking for a way out. What I really wanted was a simple faith-based program that was easy to follow and provided me with a recovery toolbox I could put use. Alcoholics Anonymous was a huge step for me. I learned a lot about living a spiritual life (more than I ever learned in church). What I really wanted was a program that would provide me with relief from alcoholism but that also was Bible-based. I could not find exactly what I was looking for, so I took what I was learning and combined that with the Bible learning I had accumulated over so many years.

It's a simple, Bible-based, and God-focused program that will bring you closer to your Creator.

God's Plan

God's plan, in one respect, is universally true. That is, He wants all people to come to a saving faith in His Son, Jesus Christ. In another respect, God's plan is unique to each of His children. He has gifted each of us with unique skills and talents that can be used to further His kingdom. However, before we can be useful to Him, we must be sober and free of addiction.

Freedom from Addiction

It sounds so easy to be free of addiction, but it's not. It's a ton of work and an ongoing process. If we let our guard down, even for a moment, Satan can and will attack. When we depend on alcohol or drugs to get through life, then by definition, we are not relying on Him. What He wants for each of us is our unfettered faith in His ability to provide for our needs. All of our needs. Not to be glib, but He wants us to be addicted to Him.

If you think back on your life of chemical addiction, how much control did your substance of choice have in your life? For me, toward the end of my alcoholism, alcohol was the most important thing in my life. Every day when I got up, I was thinking about when I would get my next drink, where I would get that drink, and how early I could leave work to get to the bar. Now, I can only imagine what my life would have been like had I put as much time into my faith as I did into my drinking.

Pathway Forward

I know we are supposed to always be looking forward. We cannot always be looking over our shoulder, or we'll never fully realize the forgiveness we have in Him. However, looking back can inform the future. If I put as much effort into my faith as I did into my drinking, the opportunities for my ministry are limitless.

As I started to focus more on faith and less on alcohol, I became a better husband, dad, child, and Christian. God has so much more use for me when I am sober. And being sober has made my life so much more rewarding. In the pages that follow, I will take you through a six-step plan to sobriety. It took me five years to write what will take you six weeks to complete. I developed this program while reflecting on my own recovery journey. Looking back over my journey, these six truths helped me find sobriety. Most importantly, they helped me maintain my sobriety and learn what God has in store for me.

Commit to the Journey   ● ● ●

I hope you take this six-week journey. You can make it your own. Each day offers you an opportunity to record what you are learning and how your life is changing because of the principles you read in the Bible. Each week may be downloaded in .pdf format from ProjectSobriety.com, where there are moderated forums that discuss each of these principles.

Engage with the Program   ● ● ●

I hope you engage with the program. If you work at least as hard at your faith as you did at feeding your addiction, you will see unbelievable results. Perhaps the greatest takeaway is that God cares for you, no matter what you have done. He stands ready to forgive you and welcome you into His family, and best of all, He can and will use you to further His kingdom. The rewards are beyond description. I hope God uses these resources to impact your life in a meaningful way along your journey to recovery. Now, let's look at the program.

The problem I had with using church as a program of recovery is that few Christians involved in the churches around me were struggling with addiction. The adage "It takes one to know one" really applies here. If you've never struggled with addiction, you won't have the life experience and related tools to help a recovering addict. I am a Christian who struggles with addiction, so I get it. What you will find here is the plan of recovery that has really helped me.

Pathway to Recovery Program   ● ● ●

Pathway to Recovery is an addiction recovery program that is faith-based and practical. The program is based on six recovery steps designed to provide addicts with a recovery toolbox they need to succeed. There are also three support steps designed to provide family and friends of the addict with a recovery support toolbox they need to support the addict's recovery plan.

Each addiction recovery program step takes one week to complete. Each week deals with one aspect of faith-based recovery, and each day focuses on one verse related to the step for that week. At the end of this initial program of recovery, you will have a deeper understanding of six key areas of the Christian faith that will help you in your recovery. Over the six weeks, you will learn forty-two verses that will provide you with a recovery toolbox to aid in your recovery.

Here are the six steps:

Step 1. Reconciliation
Step 2. Repentance
Step 3. Faith
Step 4. God's Armor
Step 5. Seek Shelter
Step 6. Run the Race

My Testimony

My story is all too common. It begins with a long slow descent into the depths of addiction, followed by a long road back to recovery. My addiction resulted from many problems and difficulties. I tried my hardest to push everyone away. I did not like who I had become and preferred to be left alone. The only place where I felt like I truly fit in was sitting in my usual chair at my usual bar. I did this six days each week. The only reason it was not seven is that the bar was closed on Sunday. I thought I had friends at the bar, but the truth is that they only liked me because I tipped well and bought drinks for those around me. Not a single person at the bar knew how to get in touch with me, unless I stopped in for a drink.

While I was in college, through the leading of a couple of close friends and my study of God's Word, I accepted the sacrifice He made on my behalf and opened my life to Him. But then the world got in the way, and things got complicated. Life got tough for me, and rather than continuing to look to God for strength and seek the answers in His Word, I got mad at everyone and everything around me. I began spending less time with God's Word and more time with my dear friend, alcohol. Alcohol provided temporary respites from the difficulties of life. But those respites were exactly that: temporary. Eventually, life caught up with me, and God reminded me who was really in charge.

I thought I was on top of the world and had life under control.

The Impact of Faith in My Life　● ● ●

I became a believer during the semester break of my freshman year in college. During my first year in college, three pivotal events occurred in my life. First, over the Christmas break, one of my best friends from high school was involved in a fatal ATV accident. He hit a tree, landed in a creek, and was dead on impact. A few weeks later, my grandmother died after a long illness. In less than two months, I had been the pallbearer at two funerals. This was a lot for me, and I was not handling it well.

At my buddy's funeral, I learned that after we graduated, he read the Bible from cover to cover. He did not come from what I thought of as a "churched" family. I did come from a churched family but spent my time drinking and having fun. After his funeral, I spent every free moment reading the Bible; I had received one nearly ten years earlier for my Presbyterian confirmation classes. Unlike my friend, I started in the New Testament.

During high school and college, I worked for a godly man and woman who owned a golf course. I was one of the few allowed to work all year. This couple treated me like a son. For me, I had two sets of parents, and frankly, that's what it took to keep me out of major trouble. A few weeks after my friend's funeral, my grandmother died. After the funeral, my friend and employer sat me down. He could tell I was struggling and wanted to talk. He took me through the Romans Road, and I became a Christian. I knew immediately that this faith was what I needed. I became a believer, and my life began to change for the good.

Lifetime Struggle ● ● ●

Like so many, I took my first drink at a very young age. I was fifteen. I drank during high school and college. Drinking continued on and off until I was in my early thirties. I didn't know this then, but I know now that alcohol came to control my life. We all have a throne in our life. There can only be one person or thing that occupies that seat at any one time. For several years, I thought I was allowing God to sit on the throne in my life.

I paid lip service to that commitment. I had not truly yielded to God. Even though I was active in my church, teaching Sunday school, writing Bible studies, and holding various positions of leadership in the church, I had not yielded my life completely to God. I put on a good show for those around me. Outwardly, it looked like I was allowing God to lead my life. Inside was a completely different story. I was dealing with anger, depression, and anxiety. I was giving God credit for the things that were happening in my life, but in my heart, I was taking credit for all my successes.

We can carry this illusion on for a time, but eventually, it will catch up with us. When I started running out of answers and things started going badly, I blamed God. Rather than looking to God for answers, I looked the other way. When I thought God didn't have answers and I didn't have answers, I turned to alcohol. I self-medicated and drank with a vengeance. Satan is wickedly and expertly deceptive that way. He began putting thoughts in my mind that God did not understand me or care about me. After all, if He cared for me, why would He allow me to begin to crash and burn? God wants to protect me from the deceptive ways of Satan. Gradually, however, Satan began planting little seeds that God really did not care. As things got worse, Satan changed his tactics and began to convince me that God could never use a person like me. I had become a prodigal.

Satan's deception caused me to experience a level of hopelessness and loneliness that I did not think was possible to live through.

Early Life   ● ● ●

As a child, I grew up in a home where church was important. We attended church most Sundays. After I turned eighteen, however, church and its teachings became less important. I rebelled for a time and wandered from God through the last part of high school and the first part of college. During Christmas break of my freshman year in college, I returned to Him after a couple of significant deaths in my life. Those deaths caused me to see a need for Jesus and what He could do in a life committed to Him.

I walked by faith, or at least thought I was walking by faith, for the next decade. My foundation of faith was not as strong as I thought. Eventually, my faith was put to the test, and I failed in spectacular fashion. When the going got tough, I got going. I wandered from God at the exact point in my life when I should have been leaning on Him more. After checking into rehab, I returned to the faith I had once cultivated in God.

I am living proof that there is a loving God, that the power of prayer is real, and that true change can occur when family and friends refuse to give up.

Early Career and Family Life ● ● ●

By the time I reached my late twenties, I had become the chief financial officer of a large hospital that treated people with addictions (ironically, I checked into the same hospital twenty years later for treatment for alcoholism). I left the hospital after three years. Over the next decade and a half, I changed jobs every four or five years. Each new job offered more responsibility than the one before it. In my late thirties, I became the chief executive officer of an orthopedic specialty hospital. When I was thirty-nine, I made the Forty Under 40 class of 2006 in Indianapolis. The following year, I became the chief executive officer of the hospital's corporate parent. By all outward appearances, I had it together, and my trajectory was straight up. I never imagined making it that far in such a short amount of time.

During the time my career was taking off, things appeared to be going well at home. We had three beautiful daughters and had built our dream house in a nice neighborhood. I was also very active in my local church. I taught Sunday school, was a finance committee member, served on the board of deacons, and wrote high school Bible studies for our church.

In June of 2012, I left the company to start a consulting business. By the time I left, the organization had doubled in size through the worst economy in recorded history and had grown to over nine hundred employees. What could go wrong? I thought I was bulletproof. Outwardly, everything was looking up.

Inwardly, I knew things were headed for a crash landing, but I simply didn't know how to ask for help.

Life Unhinged ● ● ●

Within two years of starting my business, the veneer cracked. I moved out of my house and into a condominium, thoroughly ruining a summer for my wife, my kids, and my family. Life had broken me, and I took it out on everyone around me. There was no good reason to do so, but my wife continued to contact me and pray for me despite the terrible things I had said and done to her. She gave me my space, but also maintained contact. She and DWF, a close friend, unleashed an unrelenting prayer attack on me. I did not want prayer. As a matter of fact, I told them not to pray for me. I was not sure prayer would work, even if they tried. They prayed for me anyway. I did not realize at the time how pivotal this would be in an otherwise tumultuous and miserable summer.

Life-Changing Event ● ● ●

In 2014, I hit my rock bottom. I was on the verge of losing everything. My drinking was out of control; alcohol had become my greatest nemesis. On September 12, 2014, after a series of events, I entered rehab. The following day was my first totally alcohol-free day in a very long time. I left rehab on September 17 and received another chance at life. Faith in a power greater than myself has given me that chance. My higher power higher power is God. I am living proof that God, through His Son Jesus, can rescue anyone. He rescued me from my very lowest point in life. If He can rescue me, He can rescue anyone.

I never want to forget the depths I had fallen to, and I never want to return. I enjoy the view from the peaks of life rather than the valleys. In 2014, I was looking for a port in the worst storm of my life. I found that port in returning to God's Word and to Jesus. The Pathway to Recovery pathway to addiction recovery is the plan God has used to facilitate my personal recovery. I hope my story and this program help you find your port with Him as well.

He is the one true port in any storm.

Course Correction ● ● ●

On September 12, 2014, my life changed course dramatically. I hit rock bottom. Throughout all those years of perceived success, a dark secret loomed within me, a secret few if any recognized, a secret I was unwilling to share with anyone, not even my family or closest friends. Alcohol had taken control of my life. At this point, I was drinking at least a fifth a day, every day. I drank when I got up in the morning, during the day when I was not working, and from mid-afternoon until whenever I finally went to sleep at night.

Some of my closest family began to express concern at my drinking. I went to Fairbanks Hospital to talk to a counselor friend of mine. I wanted to prove to my family that I really did not have a problem with alcohol. Long story short: I ended up checking into Fairbanks. I had a serious problem with alcohol; I was an alcoholic.

It was an uncertain time. I was supposed to be at family weekend at Ball State University but obviously missed that. I had been on an eight-day bender, drinking over a fifth a day, each day. During those eight days, I was drinking around the clock. I don't remember much other than I didn't leave my condo. In fact, I spent most of my time in bed or on the couch with vodka, Diet Coke, and fresh ice close at hand. I didn't want to wake up. In fact, I was angry with myself and God that I kept waking up. I didn't know which way to turn. I just wanted the pain and misery to stop.

God's Mercy ● ● ●

I was fortunate; God gave me another chance. I didn't realize how close to the line I had skated. I wanted to wait one week to check into rehab. After I sobered up, they told me I would not have survived another week. I thought it was a scared straight event until I went to my family doctor. He told me that he had three other alcoholic patients, but none of them drank as hard as me. He then told me all three had died of alcohol-related health problems. It was at that moment that I realized how close I came to death. Today, I feel better than I have in a long time. It has taken a balance of faith, family, much-needed medications, and most importantly, an unrelenting prayer attack.

With God's help, my life has been completely rebuilt. I have scaled some things back. I am focused on achieving some semblance of faith-life-work balance. There are no words to express my heartfelt thanks to those who endured this time with me. I am so grateful that they didn't give up on me. And I am extremely grateful for a loving God Who welcomed me back home. The same God Who welcomed me back home wants to welcome you to His family as well.

Make the commitment to start your journey today. You will not be disappointed. You may get started at www.ProjectSobriety.com.

STEP 1 • • • • • • • •

Reconciliation

But God shows his love for us in that while we
were still sinners, Christ died for us.
—Romans 5:8 (ESV)

Introduction to Reconciliation   • • •

Step 1 of my personal recovery process required me to understand what reconciliation means and realize that it extends to me. Toward the end of my drinking career, I did not think God could ever use me again. In my mind, I was a complete failure; I thought God had given up on me. I had a couple of people who prayed for me, even after I told them clearly to stop. I was angry with God, everyone, and everything around me. What I now realize is that God, to impress upon me how great my need is for Him, allowed me to sink to my personal rock bottom.

The Israelites wandered in the desert for forty years before they entered the Promised Land. The prodigal son had to eat from a pig trough before he humbled himself and returned to his family. I relate to the prodigal son. By the time I quit drinking, I had lost almost everything the world considers important. Through the love of God and the actions of others, I began to realize that God still had a plan for me, despite my inner turmoil. Reconciliation means that I now have a place in heaven with God, Jesus, and all those who have gone before me and will come along after me. Jesus died for me long before I was ever born. He died because of the sin He knew I would commit.

Self-Sufficiency

I had become self-sufficient. I didn't think I needed God or anyone else to help me out. In my mind, I couldn't rely on anyone else to help me with my problems. I felt I had to deal with my inner demons on my own. Eventually, I came to understand that I needed help. I had to want that help; that's not as easy as it sounds. Not many people saw my dark side, but those who did knew I was sick. They were unable to help me because I didn't want to help myself. I'm not proud of this, but I was extremely skilled at hiding my dark side from others. I mastered the art of deception. On the rare event someone tried to call me out, I simply changed the subject.

Rock Bottom

We all must hit rock bottom before we can begin the recovery process. Rock bottom is different for everyone. When I hit my rock bottom, I began to realize that I might need help. I wasn't convinced, but I was beginning to listen.

Part of step 1 for me was to go to Fairbanks Hospital for an assessment; I met with the only person in the city I trusted, and after only a couple of minutes, she determined that I was sick and needed to check into the hospital. I honestly thought she might suggest I do outpatient detox and group therapy. I was not there to check in. I didn't even bring an overnight bag. I was there to prove everyone else wrong.

Fortunately, they saw in me what I could not see in myself: that alcohol had taken over every aspect of my life.

The Reconciliation Process

What does this have to do with reconciliation? I needed to come to the realization that reconciliation was extended even to someone like me. In terms of my faith, I am a two-time loser who never thought God would ever use me again. I had so much spiritually, yet I threw it all away for the sake of the next bottle of liquor.

The reconciliation that God provides through His Son forced me to think outside myself. Addicts are self-absorbed people who believe they can beat almost anything. I eventually came to accept the fact that I couldn't beat this on my own. I needed a power greater than myself if I was going to beat the odds. So many told me how bad off I was.

My Reality ● ● ●

I really wanted to leave and return to Fairbanks the following Friday. I was involved in a transaction that was about to close. My friend convinced me the transaction could wait, so I checked in. My first day in rehab, I was told three times that I likely would not have survived until the following Friday. That's a shocker for anyone to hear. I thought they were pulling the Scared Straight routine on me. However, they told my wife the exact same thing. And to top it all off, one of my doctors told me that people who fell as low as I did had the odds of recovery stacked heavily against them.

After I came to terms with the fact that I needed to stay at the treatment center, I realized how close my brush with death had really been. Most people who drank like I did would die of alcohol poisoning. My final bender lasted eight days. During that time, I drank twenty-two hours per day. I couldn't even drink myself to sleep. I slept maybe two hours per day. When I was picked up to go to the assessment center, my blood alcohol level was already 0.16—twice the legal limit to drive—and it was only noon.

The Beginning of Healing ● ● ●

My road to recovery began when I realized that God could forgive a person like me. In fact, He had already provided for my reconciliation and was waiting for me to decide to return to His family. I had come full circle. I felt like I was getting back many of the gifts I had left behind. Bible verses are came back to me. Passages are came back to me. And critical verse linkages came back to me. God extended me grace to return to Him.

Keys to Reconciliation   ● ● ●

Reconciliation for me involved three key understandings:

God Loves Us: First and foremost, I had to come to terms with the fact that God loves even me. There is not one thing I could do that would permanently separate me from God, other than never surrendering to Him.

Surrender: I had to admit that I no longer controlled alcohol; it controlled me. I had to give my life over to Him. He had to become the most important thing in my life. Without a power greater than myself—God—I would never have a chance to be well.

Trust: I had to admit, after forty-eight years, that I had finally run across a problem I couldn't solve on my own. For the first time in my life, I had to trust in God and others to get through the tough road ahead of me.

Closing Thoughts   ● ● ●

Romans 5:8 says, "And while we were yet sinners, Christ died for us." Christ died for me, not because of any good I had done or because of who I thought I was. He died for me despite all that baggage. Satan took me down a dark road, a road that said, "Jesus would never die for you. You tried to repent of your sins, and look where that got you. You are on the outside looking in, you are without direction, you do not fit in, and you feel abandoned by God." That is a truly hopeless feeling. I have never experienced a loneliness as intense as I did the last couple of years of my drinking. I was completely and totally isolated.

My problem was that I had the order mixed up. I am first reconciled by God to Himself through Jesus, then I repent of my sins. The order makes an enormous difference. I came to the realization that if I was going to conquer alcohol, it was going to take the help of others, most importantly, Jesus.

My doctors told me that I beat tremendous odds. One doctor told me every time I saw him that most people who find themselves where I was never climb out. I am under no illusion that I did this on my own. As soon as I walk away from the program or get a little too self-confident, I can fall right back into the abyss. I realized that I had to commit to a lifestyle of honesty, brutal honesty. If I can't be honest, I can't understand all that God has done for me, and I can never beat alcohol.

Next Steps ● ● ●

Are you ready to admit defeat? Do you feel lost? Can you see no way out? Are you ready to do anything to get your life back? Then you are ready to begin this program. The Pathway to Recovery will help you decide if you want to seek God's best for your life. He is the only One Who can provide you a sure way out of the darkness that comes with addiction.

Weekly Plan ● ● ●

- Day 12 Corinthians 5:18–20
- Day 2:Romans 5:10
- Day 3: Ephesians 2:16
- Day 4: Romans 5:11
- Day 5: Colossians 1:19–20
- Day 6: Romans 11:15
- Day 7: Romans 8:9

Day 1: 2 Corinthians 5:18–20

• • •

Prayer for Today
God, today grant me
Strength to do as You please,
Wisdom to discern Your best for me,
Compassion to serve others who need You, and
Power to overcome the world's temptations.

BIBLE VERSE

All this is from God, who through Christ reconciled us to himself
and gave us the ministry of reconciliation; that is, in Christ God was
reconciling the world to himself, not counting their trespasses against
them, and entrusting to us the message of reconciliation. Therefore,
we are ambassadors for Christ, God making his appeal through
us. We implore you on behalf of Christ, be reconciled to God.
—2 Corinthians 5:18–20 ESV

RECONCILIATION

Reconciliation with God is a concept I never really thought about. It's hard
for me to fathom that God sent His Son to die on a cross, in advance, for
sins He knew each person would commit at a future date. Christ provides
my reconciliation before I was even born. He knew I would commit sins
against His Father, yet He still provided for my reconciliation. He not
only provided for my reconciliation, He gave each of us a message of
reconciliation.

God has provided for our reconciliation. He offered the ultimate
sacrifice on our behalf.

APPLICATION

Toward the end of my drinking and at the beginning of my sobriety, I felt like I didn't deserve God's grace or His gift of reconciliation. I had failed Him completely, on every level. One of the lies Satan spreads is that because of our past, we can never be used by God in the future. Satan uses our past to convince us that we are beyond hope. For a while, I believed that lie. However, I now realize that God used scores of people throughout history to advance His kingdom. Some of the greatest people in the Bible had the worst, most violent history. Yet, when faced with God's Word and His Son, they first accepted the reconciliation offered by God and then repented of their wicked ways.

Today is a good day to accept the reconciliation offered by the one true God.

COMMITMENT

Look at how verse 20 ends: "We implore you on behalf of Christ, be reconciled to God." What a strong statement. The word *implore* sticks out to me. God is appealing to you to be reconciled to Him.

Make a commitment today to seek reconciliation with God.

PRAYER

Lord, help me today to begin to understand that You want to reconcile with me. Regardless of the things I have done, help me trust that Your reconciliation extends even to me.

JOURNAL

_____
_____
_____
_____
_____
_____
_____
_____
_____

GRATEFUL

_____
_____
_____
_____
_____
_____
_____
_____
_____

AMENDS

_____
_____
_____
_____
_____
_____
_____
_____
_____

JOHN MARTIN

Day 2: Romans 5:10

• • •

Prayer for Today
God, today grant me
Strength to do as You please,
Wisdom to discern Your best for me,
Compassion to serve others who need You, and
Power to overcome the world's temptations.
For if while we were enemies we were reconciled to
God by the death of his Son, much more, now that
we are reconciled, shall we be saved by his life.
—Romans 5:10 (ESV)

RECONCILIATION

In this one verse, we learn three facts about reconciliation:

1. Jesus provided our reconciliation while we were still His enemies.
2. He died to provide that reconciliation.
3. Our salvation is through His life and the reconciliation He offers.

The first part of this verse describes us as God's enemies. It's easy to gloss over that word and not think it through. Have you ever had an enemy? We've all had our enemies over the years. If I think about all the plans I've had to deal with my enemies, providing reconciliation and salvation has never been on the agenda. I tend to think of ways to get even. If God used my own approach on me, I would face complete and utter destruction. The second part of this verse describes the reconciliation the Lord provides. While I don't understand why death was necessary, I do understand the enormity of the sacrifice God made. He allowed His own Son to be put to death. I would fight to my own death before I allowed one of my own kids to be sacrificed. Yet that is exactly what God did.

APPLICATION

So what does this mean to me?

1. Jesus knew my evil sinful behavior even before I did.
2. Despite that, he still died for me.
3. I now have life through Him.

Think about how different the world would be today if we all took God's approach to our enemies. So much of my addiction was the result of pent-up anger. I was always trying to take care of my problems on my own, and trying to get even with the people who were my enemies. I allowed the world to completely beat me down. But God gives me a way that is so much better. How much different would my life have been if I had followed God's example. While I cannot change the past, I can certainly change the future. It makes no difference how bad I think I am or have been. He already knows and provides my reconciliation, anyway. God has given me a chance to start over; I need to be able to do the same for myself.

The challenge we face is not whether God can forgive us, but rather whether we can forgive ourselves.

COMMITMENT

Think about the reconciliation God is offering you today. Looking at my past, it is impossible to understand why God would save a sinner like me. Yet that is exactly what He has done.

I need to be thankful today for the reconciliation God as provided from eternity past.

PRAYER

Lord, thank You that even while I was still Your enemy, You provided for my reconciliation.

JOURNAL

_____
_____
_____
_____
_____
_____
_____
_____
_____
_____

GRATEFUL

_____
_____
_____
_____
_____
_____
_____
_____
_____
_____

AMENDS

_____
_____
_____
_____
_____
_____
_____
_____
_____
_____

Day 3: Ephesians 2:16

• • •

Prayer for Today
God, today grant me
Strength to do as You please,
Wisdom to discern Your best for me,
Compassion to serve others who need You, and
Power to overcome the world's temptations.
And might reconcile us both to God in one body
through the cross, thereby killing the hostility.
—Ephesians 2:16 (ESV)

RECONCILIATION

Reconciliation is what Jesus did for me before I even understood that I was separated from Him. Recall back to verse 12: We were separated, alienated, strangers, without hope, and without God. For an addict, that pretty much describes the last day before sobering up. Honestly, we are all in that spot and come to that realization for the last time on the day before we open our heart and our mind to what Christ wants to do in us and through us. Jesus was sent to this earth, by His Father, to atone for all the wrong we did in the past and will do in the future.

Notice how this verse describes the gift of reconciliation given to us. He reconciled us with one body through the cross. Jesus died for each of us. He is the Lamb, the New Testament equivalent of the lamb sacrificed for sin in the Old Testament. With one big exception: The sacrifice made by Jesus is once for all. He does not have to be sacrificed over and over.

APPLICATION

One of the hardest things for me, and I suspect for many of us, is to realize that regardless of how far I have wandered, His reconciliation still extends to me. Christ reconciled us through the cross. He is responsible for killing the hostility that we felt and that may have been directed at us. There is so much to reconciliation. When I was apart from God, it was lonely and miserable. I was lost, wandering aimlessly and convinced that God could not or would not use me. I had given up and figured this world was better without me.

Step 1 of my personal recovery process was to understand that reconciliation extends to me and realize what it means to me. It means that I now have a place in heaven with God, Jesus, and all those who have gone before me and will come along after me.

COMMITMENT

As you reflect on life while struggling with addiction, were you lonely and miserable? Did you feel like you didn't fit in or that you weren't good enough? Take time to reflect on the reconciliation God has provided each of us. Thank Him for that reconciliation, and ask Him to help you realize the impact of that reconciliation in your life.

PRAYER

Lord, thank You for the blessing of reconciliation. I have taken it for granted, and frankly, I did so when I did not fully understand the nature of reconciliation. Help me demonstrate my gratitude for reconciliation, both today and in the future.

JOURNAL

_____

_____

_____

_____

_____

_____

_____

_____

_____

GRATEFUL

_____

_____

_____

_____

_____

_____

_____

_____

_____

AMENDS

_____

_____

_____

_____

_____

_____

_____

_____

_____

JOHN MARTIN

Day 4: Romans 5:11

• • •

Prayer for Today
God, today grant me
Strength to do as You please,
Wisdom to discern Your best for me,
Compassion to serve others who need You, and
Power to overcome the world's temptations.
And not only this, but we also exult in God through our Lord Jesus
Christ, through whom we have now received the reconciliation.
—Romans 5:11 (NASB)

RECONCILIATION

Have you ever searched for something only to find it, hours later, sitting right in front of you? For many of us, that is reconciliation. We spend a very long time looking for something that's hiding right out in the open. The problem is that we think there's a great mystery associated with finding reconciliation. Because our society has drifted so far from the faith, we actually get pulled away from our answers instead of toward them.

How do you feel when you lose your keys and then find them? I know I feel a sense of relief and joy. A tremendous weight is lifted from my shoulders anytime I find something important that I've lost.

Like any other lost item, when we finally realize that we have found reconciliation, there is an immediate sense of relief and contentment.

APPLICATION

For me, I lost sight of a lot of things for a very long time. I violated my own principle: "Do what you enjoy; don't simply chase dollar bills." How I wish I followed my own advice. I started moving down the funnel slowly, but the further I went, the faster the spiral turned. I got to a point where I honestly thought my only value to this world was to make money, keep people supplied with what they need (not just family, but work as well), and keep concentrating on climbing the ladder.

It was all so hollow and intensely lonely. What I really needed was not a raise but a reminder that I first need reconciliation.

Commitment

Take time this week to begin to set your priorities straight. Too often, our motivation is selfishness. We don't think others can help us. The more we rely on self, the worse our problem becomes. Take time to slow down and consider your priorities. Use the reconciliation God offers to begin to align your priorities with His.

Prayer

Lord, help me to live my life today for You and in light of what You have done for me. We have an opportunity to praise God, and that only comes through the reconciliation we have received from You.

JOURNAL

_____
_____
_____
_____
_____
_____
_____
_____
_____

GRATEFUL

_____
_____
_____
_____
_____
_____
_____
_____
_____

AMENDS

_____
_____
_____
_____
_____
_____
_____
_____
_____

Day 5: Colossians 1:19–20

● ● ●

Prayer for Today
God, today grant me
Strength to do as You please,
Wisdom to discern Your best for me,
Compassion to serve others who need You, and
Power to overcome the world's temptations.
For in him all the fullness of God was pleased to dwell, and
through him to reconcile to himself all things, whether on
earth or in heaven, making peace by the blood of his cross.
—Colossians 1:19-20 (ESV)

RECONCILIATION

Reconciliation can be a difficult concept to understand. There is so much evil, disease, crime, and despair all around us. It is hard to imagine that there is a loving God Who is in control. But there is. He is in control and wants each of us to come to our own personal relationship with Him. He is not going to force Himself on us, but He will always make Himself available to us.

When I take the time to think about all of nature's intricacies and moving parts, I cannot help but believe our world was created by intelligent design. There is no possible way that we just came to exist. There is a cascade of events we must be fully aware of: 1. God created the heavens and the earth. 2. He created each of us. 3. He is full of love, goodness, righteousness, and justice. 4. He reconciled each of us to Himself through His Son, Jesus. 5. And through the reconciliation of His Son, we may each experience His fullness.

As I look back on the last fifteen years, what I really needed was hope, peace, and reconciliation. I was making a very common mistake; I was looking in all the wrong places. Nothing was sticking. I knew I needed something more. I didn't realize that I could not experience the former two until I experienced the latter. Without Jesus, nothing we experience here is lasting. Do you think your problems are too big? Do you think you made one mistake too many, or the one you made crosses some line of no return? That is Satan scraping around your armor, looking for any opening, no matter how small, so that he can exploit that gap and cause you to experience doubt.

APPLICATION

It is easy to fall victim to the "why me?" syndrome. Why me? What have I done to deserve His love, reconciliation, and salvation? The answer: I have done absolutely nothing. I receive all He has to offer because it is His gift to me. And why not me? God has already provided for my reconciliation, even knowing the sinful things I would do even before I did them. Even with that knowledge, He still loves me enough to provide me a pathway to Himself. Why would I not accept such a valuable gift?

Instead, we should consider the phrase "Why not me?"

I cannot drive home the point enough, that what we receive and what we become begins with reconciliation. You may ask how we experience reconciliation; I know I did. The fantastic news is that the price was already paid. From before we were born, before we knew about sin, while we were still His enemies, He died to reconcile us to Himself. Through Him, we have been reconciled. Through Him and through His blood, we receive peace.

Look at how Jesus is described in Colossians 1:15–18. He had everything yet gave up everything on our behalf.

COMMITMENT

Begin your walk today, grateful that God has given you the gift of reconciliation. That gift came at a tremendous cost to the Father. He paid that price specifically for you, knowing what is in your past. He wants you to rest in the peace and comfort that you may only experience in the knowledge that you have been reconciled by a God Who loves you deeply.

PRAYER

Lord, help me to understand that while there are many difficulties on this earth, nothing can separate us from Your love and the reconciliation that You offer to each of us.

JOURNAL

_____
_____
_____
_____
_____
_____
_____
_____
_____
_____

GRATEFUL

_____
_____
_____
_____
_____
_____
_____
_____
_____
_____

AMENDS

_____
_____
_____
_____
_____
_____
_____
_____
_____
_____

Day 6: Romans 11:15

● ● ●

Prayer for Today
God, today grant me
Strength to do as You please,
Wisdom to discern Your best for me,
Compassion to serve others who need You, and
Power to overcome the world's temptations.
For if their rejection is the reconciliation of the world,
what will their acceptance be but life from the dead?
—Romans 11:15 (NASB)

RECONCILIATION

Death can mean a lot of things, but reconciliation? In Old Testament times, Israel turned its back on God over and over again. As a result, through His Son Jesus, God brought the message of salvation to the gentiles. Why is that so important? Because if Israel had not rejected God, our pathway to salvation could have been much different. The gentiles were the unholy, irreligious side of society, at least according to the religious leaders of the time. The Pharisees and other religious leaders thought themselves to be on a spiritual plane far above the gentiles. The religious leaders followed the law to the letter, or so they thought. And they looked down on and talked down to the lowly gentiles.

APPLICATION

So why is this so important to the chemically addicted? Because, at least in my case, I began to feel like the gentiles. Everywhere I looked, I saw people that were better than me. They had it together. I was coming unglued. As the days went by, I was feeling a greater sense of loneliness and isolation. I felt like I was alone and that no one understood my predicament, not even God. Looking back, I could not have been more wrong. Whether I wanted to admit it or not, God was right there waiting. All I needed to do was ask Him for help. But I could not do that. At the time I felt as though I were too far gone, and He would not want anything to do with me. I could not have been more wrong! I needed to put away self-pity and pride and ask God for help. I was able to do that once the chemicals left my body and I began to think straight again.

COMMITMENT

Are you feeling a deep sense of being alone and isolated? Take that first step toward God. The Father is right there next to you, waiting for you to walk toward Him and ask Him for help. Start your day today by asking God to replace your emptiness with His goodness.

PRAYER

Lord, today help me to understand that You are there, waiting for me to lean on You for help. Help me to put away self, ask for help, and trust You to deliver me from the problems I face.

JOURNAL

_____
_____
_____
_____
_____
_____
_____
_____
_____

GRATEFUL

_____
_____
_____
_____
_____
_____
_____
_____
_____

AMENDS

_____
_____
_____
_____
_____
_____
_____
_____
_____

Day 7: Romans 8:9

• • •

Prayer for Today
God, today grant me
Strength to do as You please,
Wisdom to discern Your best for me,
Compassion to serve others who need You, and
Power to overcome the world's temptations.
You, however, are not in the flesh but in the Spirit, if in
fact the Spirit of God dwells in you. Anyone who does not
have the Spirit of Christ does not belong to him.
—Romans 8:9 (ESV)

RECONCILIATION

Have you come to terms with reconciliation? It is a tough concept to grasp at first. No one ever cleared a path for me before I even thought about walking that path. No one ever made the sacrifices for me like Christ has made.

The first key decision in the pathway to recovery is deciding to turn the care of my life over to a Person Who is greater than me. If I am willing to accept the reconciliation God offers me, then my life changes forever, in a good way. In this verse, Paul tells us that if we are willing to accept the reconciliation offered by God, then we are no longer His enemy. We now belong to Him. There is now a spiritual aspect to my life that was not there before.

Reconciliation is the first step in the journey along the path of faith-based recovery.

APPLICATION

The only way I was ever able to deal with my addiction was by taking that first step. It was a biggie. For the first time in my life, I was required to step out on faith. I came to the realization that I needed to rely on someone outside of myself to help me along the way. That Someone is God. In addition to being outside of me (in an earthly, tangible sense), I could not experience God with my five senses (sight, touch, hearing, smell, and taste). In a very real way, I had to rely on a sixth sense, a spiritual sense, that was beyond anything I could imagine.

Step 1. Reconciliation: For the first time in my life, I was required to step out on faith. I am no longer living for me. I am living for a much greater purpose.

COMMITMENT

The first decision you need to make as part of a faith-based recovery program is, are you willing to accept the reconciliation that God is offering through His Son, Jesus? When the answer to that question is yes, then you're ready to take the next step.

PRAYER

Lord, strengthen me and strengthen my faith today. Shelter me as I face this evil world. I thank You, Lord, for Your tent that You use to conceal me until the time is right for me to fulfill Your calling on my life.

Journal

_____
_____
_____
_____
_____
_____
_____
_____

Grateful

_____
_____
_____
_____
_____
_____
_____
_____

Amends

_____
_____
_____
_____
_____
_____
_____
_____
_____

Repentance

The Intent of the Heart ● ● ●

Step 2 requires us to look at the topic of repentance and ask how we can repent of the actions that have brought us to this place. In Acts 8:9–22, we are told the story of a man named Simon, who had been a magician. The implication is that he no longer practiced magic, and during this passage, we discover why he abandoned the practice. The people throughout the land of Samaria were amazed by the magic Simon practiced. They thought he was great because of his magic. They paid attention to him because of his magic. It amazed them. They paid attention less on the results of what he was doing and more on him. I am sure this fed into how Simon thought of himself. He was clearly popular, and as the verses continue, I get the impression he liked the attention that went with his acts of magic.

Simon's Change

Then things began to change. Philip came to Samaria and began preaching the Gospel. The people responded favorably to Philip's message. After the people heard this message, they were moved and became baptized. They changed their way of thinking. They were not as amazed by Simon and his magic because they had seen a better way. The message delivered by Philip was clearly compelling and moving, because even Simon himself believed Philip's message.

Simon was moved by the message delivered by Philip and the miracles he was performing.

As a result of seeing Philip's faith in action, Simon wanted to know what he could do to receive the same ability. Clearly, the message did not sink in completely because Simon tried to buy the same power from the apostles. Simon wanted to purchase the ability to perform miracles. Peter quickly set Simon straight. Peter dealt firmly with Simon, telling him that the ability to perform miracles was not for sale. Simon was sent away by Peter with a very clear message that he needed to get his heart right with God, repent, and ask the Lord for His forgiveness.

Comparison to Simon

Are we really all that different from Simon? If we are completely honest, we would have to say no, we are no different. I know my first reaction when facing any problem is to try to fix it. In our culture, we tend to believe that we can spend our way out of most problems. We leave no room for God to work. Prayer is often our last resort rather than our primary tool against difficulties and attacks by Satan.

How much different would my life be if my first reaction to every circumstance was to ask God for His help instead of trying to figure things out on my own?

Moving from Realization to Mobilization   ● ● ●

Reconciliation is a step of realization. Perhaps for the first time in life, addicts realize that there is a greater plan in life. They realize that someone else has already done for them what they could not do for themselves. For me, I began to realize that Satan was using my past to condemn me. His weapon of choice was the constant accusation that I was not good enough for God. How could God use a broken and flawed vessel to achieve His unbroken and unflawed plan? Satan sowed a message of hopelessness and despair. And he's really good at it.

The next step in my recovery was critical: to move from realization to mobilization. I came to realize that God had provided for my reconciliation, but now I needed to do something about it. I needed to mobilize my newfound knowledge. The pathway to mobilization is repentance. I desperately needed to take responsibility for my shortcomings and my sins. The way to do that is to repent. I needed to make a conscious decision to change my heart, my mind, and my actions.

Could I Change?

Over time, God demonstrated to me that I could change, but I had to want it. I had to realize that the Lord would give me the strength to make some very difficult life changes. God gives each of us a chance to be a new creature, but to take advantage of that opportunity, we are required to make meaningful lifestyle changes.

He gives each of us a chance to put our past behind us, but the hardest part of that change is to admit my own personal shortcomings and sins. No one else can do that for me.

What Is Repentance?

In Step 1, we saw that God provided for our reconciliation since the beginning of time because He knew we would make bad decisions that would ultimately lead to death. Because He provides the gift of reconciliation, we have an opportunity to live eternally with Him if we receive that gift.

How am I to receive the gift of reconciliation? Through the process of repentance. Why is repentance a process? It is a process because it never ends until we depart this world to spend eternity with Him. Certainly, we hope and expect that we will not be constantly entangled in the same sin, over and over. Part of life, however, is continuing to grow into our faith. The way we grow into our faith is to become aware of new areas where we need to repent and change the way we live. Each time God reveals to us an area where we've been wrong, we must repent of that wrong behavior and change the way we live going forward.

Repentance Is a Gateway

If repentance is the gateway to meaningful and lasting life change, then how am I to repent? The dictionary defines repentance as "the action or process of repenting especially for misdeeds or moral shortcomings https://www. merriam-webster.com/dictionary/repentance." Merriam-Webster's goes on to define *repenting* as "to turn from sin and dedicate oneself to the amendment of one's life https://www.merriam-webster.com/dictionary/repenting."

The key is not in looking back at who we were and what we did, but rather who God is changing us into over the course of time.

What Must I Do?

It is clear that God calls us to repent of our sins so we may receive His gift of reconciliation. True repentance is a process that includes at least four steps:

- spend time with God in His Word and in prayer
- allow Him to show us where we fall short or cause harm to ourselves or others
- seek His guidance in how to resolve our shortcomings
- repent: ask for forgiveness, turn from sin, commit to follow Him

God provides so much for us, but we do have to act. We cannot fix our problems on our own; that is clear from the examples provided to us in the Bible. The action require of us is one of mobilization.

We must take what we have learned and put it into action by repenting, asking for forgiveness of sin, and (most importantly) changing the way we live because of what we've learned.

Words and Actions

When we are evaluated by the people around us, it is less by what we say than it is by what we do. It is very true that our actions speak far louder than our words.

The true evidence of a life changed by repentance is a life that does not continue to walk in the way of sin.

It is more than how we act when we are in public. Probably a greater indicator of true repentance is how we think, act, and behave when we believe we are alone. We are never truly alone. God is always with us. Is what I think or do in private pleasing to God? If it is, then what I say and do in public is more likely to be pleasing to Him.

Weekly Plan ● ● ●

- Day 1: Acts 8:22
- Day 2: Matthew 4:17
- Day 3: Luke 13:3
- Day 4: Acts 2:38
- Day 5: Mark 1:14–15
- Day 6: Romans 2:4
- Day 7: 2 Corinthians 7:10

Day 1: Acts 8:22

● ● ●

Prayer for Today

God, today grant me
Strength to do as You please,
Wisdom to discern Your best for me,
Compassion to serve others who need You, and
Power to overcome the world's temptations.

BIBLE VERSE

Repent, therefore, of this wickedness of yours, and pray to the Lord
that, if possible, the intent of your heart may be forgiven you.
—Acts 8:22 (ESV)

REPENT

Why repent? As we have seen, we are all sinners. While we were still in that
condition, Christ died for each and every one of us so we could be reconciled
to Him. I may not realize that I commit wicked acts, but I do. And my wicked
acts are not just bad behavior. My wicked acts bear witness to the darkness that
lives in my heart. I have had to learn that it is the intent of my heart to do the
wicked things that I do. Now I must realize that the only way for me to escape
that evil is to repent. Our Father made a huge sacrifice for the sinfulness of my
ways. Who am I to turn away a gift that comes at such a high price?

Reconciliation is what God offers me. Repentance is what I do to
accept that gift.

APPLICATION

It is easy to look back, read a passage, and question why a person would
even think they could act a certain way. In this case, in Acts 8:18–19, why

did Simon think he could purchase the power the apostles derived from God? When I look back on my own life, there are plenty of times I thought I could purchase my way through. I really thought I could solve all my problems with money. If I could make just a little more, then I could solve a particular problem. But what if I had put that same energy into trusting God instead of trying to solve things on my own?

We each have a gift or gifts that God has attributed to us. To find these gifts, we must trust and follow Him. This is not something we can find on our own. He has already given us the gift, but we need to ensure that our heart is right before Him. We have all fallen into the trap Simon fell into. I tend to forget that any time I try to do things on my own, without God, my actions become wicked.

And God only defines sin, not degrees of sin.

COMMITMENT

While our sinful actions clearly require repentance, the intent of the heart that led to the action in the first place must be addressed. Make a commitment today to ask God to forgive not just your sinful actions but the sinful intent of your heart as well.

By studying reconciliation, I learned that there is a better way. Through repentance, I acknowledge that I have a problem and intend to do something to resolve it.

PRAYER

Lord, help me to learn what it means to repent and follow You. Teach me to repent, not just of my sinful actions but of the sinful intent of my heart as well.

JOURNAL

_____
_____
_____
_____
_____
_____
_____
_____
_____
_____

GRATEFUL

_____
_____
_____
_____
_____
_____
_____
_____
_____
_____

AMENDS

_____
_____
_____
_____
_____
_____
_____
_____
_____
_____

Day 2: Matthew 4:17

• • •

Prayer for Today
God, today grant me
Strength to do as You please,
Wisdom to discern Your best for me,
Compassion to serve others who need You, and
Power to overcome the world's temptations.
From that time Jesus began to preach, saying, "Repent,
for the kingdom of heaven is at hand."
—Matthew 4:17 (ESV)

REPENT

From the beginning of His ministry here on earth, the message of Jesus has been our need to repent. But why repentance? Because our nature is to do those things that are displeasing to Him. Paul describes our nature perfectly in Romans 7:15–20. Verse 15b says, "For I do not do what I want, but I do the very thing I hate." When I'm about to do something that's displeasing to God, I have a pretty good idea that I shouldn't do it. Unfortunately, I often do it anyway. That is rebellion, against God and Jesus, pure and simple.

From the beginning, He also warned that the kingdom of heaven was close at hand. His admonition to us is that we have no idea when He will return to this earth to collect His followers, so we must live as though He is coming today. Most, if not all, of my sin begins when I become so self-focused and so self-absorbed that my first thought is me and my last thought is Jesus.

Would I do the things I do if I were truly living my life as though Jesus would return today?

APPLICATION

How many times have I said, "I went to my solution of last resort, and I prayed about the matter"? Why is prayer not our line of first resort?

If focusing on God, and focusing on prayer, and seeking out God to understand how He wants us to handle certain situations is first in life, then that limits the amount of time we'll have to repent. When I am at my worst, it is generally when I have relegated something else to first in my life. The trick is to figure out what is in first place in my life and repent.

COMMITMENT

Make a commitment today to pray first in every situation and then follow where God leads. Do not allow prayer to become your last resort; make it your first resort. Prayer and seeking God must become your first line of defense. When you fail, you must repent immediately.

PRAYER

Lord, today help me to put You first in everything I do and to repent when I fail to do so.

Journal

_____
_____
_____
_____
_____
_____
_____
_____
_____

Grateful

_____
_____
_____
_____
_____
_____
_____
_____
_____

Amends

_____
_____
_____
_____
_____
_____
_____
_____
_____

Day 3: Luke 13:3

• • •

Prayer for Today
God, today grant me
Strength to do as You please
Wisdom to discern Your best for me
Compassion to serve others who need You
Power to overcome the world's temptations

BIBLE VERSE

No, I tell you; but unless you repent, you will all likewise perish.
—Luke 13:3 (ESV)

REPENT

Repentance is extremely important. God doesn't want anyone to perish, but He is also just and requires repentance for salvation. Without repentance, we will perish like any other unbeliever. It is never too late to repent, but the sooner we do, the more rewarding our life will be. Leading a rewarding life is very different from leading an easy life. An easy life is not necessarily an option, whether you live a Christ-like life or not.

APPLICATION

The question is not *if* we will have difficulty, but *when* we will have difficulty. When difficult times come, how do we handle them? How do we prepare ourselves now for that imminent encounter with the daily challenge of life? Remember the accounting of the life of the prodigal son? I lived that life. It was miserable. It was as miserable as anything I've ever experienced. Rather than repent and turn the difficulties of my life over to God, I chose to handle those challenges on my own. I handled them by drinking, and the fewer answers I found, the more I drank. I created a true death spiral for myself. And it was completely of my own making.

Then I found myself in the position of the prodigal and realized that regardless of anything prior, God loves me and truly wants the best for me. But His best also comes on His terms. I ignored His terms, and so I had to repent. I repented, but life did not get any easier; in fact, it got harder. But I no longer have to go it alone.

COMMITMENT

Repentance is always on my mind. Had Jesus not provided for my reconciliation and then given me an opportunity to repent, I would be lost and without hope of any kind. I need to commit to turning the difficulties of life over to God at first opportunity, not after I have batted it away and run out of any other options.

PRAYER

Lord, help me to understand the true meaning of what it is to truly repent of my sins. Give me the strength today to repent, to forsake my former ways, and to follow You.

JOURNAL

_____
_____
_____
_____
_____
_____
_____
_____
_____

GRATEFUL

_____
_____
_____
_____
_____
_____
_____
_____
_____

AMENDS

_____
_____
_____
_____
_____
_____
_____
_____
_____

Day 4: Acts 2:38

* * *

Prayer for Today
God, today grant me
Strength to do as You please,
Wisdom to discern Your best for me,
Compassion to serve others who need You, and
Power to overcome the world's temptations.

BIBLE VERSE

And Peter said to them, "Repent and be baptized every one
of you in the name of Jesus Christ for the forgiveness of your
sins, and you will receive the gift of the Holy Spirit."
—Acts 2:38 (ESV)

REPENT

Repenting requires me to know that I'm not right with God, that I've
done something wrong, and that I'm willing to confess that wrong and
desire to turn from it. Asking for forgiveness requires that I first admit I
have somehow wronged God or others. And that requires humility. It is
not easy to admit that I have been wrong. Also, when the Holy Spirit is
offered to us, it is a gift, not a right. Too many times today, we believe that
everything is a right, like society owes us something.

Salvation, forgiveness, and true release from sin only come as a gift
from Jesus to us.

APPLICATION

As hard as it can be to repent, the long-term benefit is so much better.
When I am able to repent and ask forgiveness, I feel as though a weight

is lifted. I now feel free to do what I couldn't do before. Of course, this also reminds me that I cannot do life alone. I need God's forgiveness and guidance. And I need the friendship of others. As you read this verse, realize that there are two things you must do and two things you will receive.

If I am willing to repent and be baptized, then I will receive the forgiveness of sins and the gift of the Holy Spirit.

I really need the gift of the Holy Spirit, but I will only receive that gift if I first recognize my sinfulness, repent, and seek forgiveness.

We must always remember that receiving the Holy Spirit is a gift, not a right.

COMMITMENT

Are you willing to admit that you are not right with God? Being able to repent requires that I know that I'm not right with God, that I've done something wrong, and that I'm willing to confess that wrong and turn away from it. Repentance is not a magic bullet; rather, it is an opportunity to set your life straight. A tremendous burden is lifted when you finally commit to repentance and ask God's forgiveness. Repentance is an early step in finally being able to live a life free of addiction and other burdens.

PRAYER

Lord, today help me to realize that the Holy Spirit is a gift, not a right. You owe me nothing. I owe You everything. Except You made the ultimate sacrifice and wiped my slate clean, as a gift.

Journal

_____
_____
_____
_____
_____
_____
_____
_____
_____

Grateful

_____
_____
_____
_____
_____
_____
_____
_____
_____

Amends

_____
_____
_____
_____
_____
_____
_____
_____
_____

Day 5: Mark 1:14–15

● ● ●

Prayer for Today
God, today grant me
Strength to do as You please,
Wisdom to discern Your best for me,
Compassion to serve others who need You, and
Power to overcome the world's temptations.

BIBLE VERSE

Now after John was arrested, Jesus came into Galilee, proclaiming
the gospel of God, and saying, "The time is fulfilled, and the
kingdom of God is at hand; repent and believe in the gospel."
—Mark 1:14–15 (ESV)

REPENT

When I repent, it is a conscious act on my part. I realize I have done
something wrong, something that is displeasing to God. I know I need
to change my ways. Repentance is a three-step process. First, I come to
understand that I've done something that could separate me from God.
Second, I must humble myself, admit my wrong, and ask God to forgive
me. Too often, I stop after the second step. It is not good enough to simply
acknowledge my wrongdoing and ask God to forgive me. I must act based
on that understanding and request forgiveness.

What is the action I need to take? The third step in the repentance
process is to turn from the evil that entangles me and leave that sin behind.
Once I have repented, I need to believe in the gospel.

I need to put my faith into action: turn from Satan, believe in the
Gospel, and run toward God.

APPLICATION

What is required of me when I repent?

In Acts 26:18, I am instructed to turn from the darkness that comes with following Satan and turn to the light that God provides after we repent of our sins. It is in the act of turning from the darkness (Satan) to the light (God) that I receive the forgiveness I so desperately need. Peter, in his first letter, tells me in chapter 3 verse 11, what I need to do in very simple and straightforward terms. In this verse, Peter tells me that I must "turn away from evil and do good; … seek peace and pursue it." These two verses tell me exactly what I need to do.

I not only need to ask for forgiveness; I must also change my ways to receive the forgiveness God offers.

COMMITMENT

Once you have repented of your sins and atoned for your wrongdoing, you must make an effort to "turn away from evil and do good; … seek peace and pursue it." Are you at that point? In 1 Peter, Peter tells us that this is one key to living a life that's pleasing to God and rewarding for us. You must commit yourself, today, to leave sin behind and pursue God and His desire for your life.

PRAYER

Lord, help me to both repent of the evil things that I do and to believe in You and Your Gospel. I know Satan is around every corner, seeking to destroy us. Help me to trust in you, my Rock and my Redeemer.

Journal

_____
_____
_____
_____
_____
_____
_____
_____
_____

Grateful

_____
_____
_____
_____
_____
_____
_____
_____
_____

Amends

_____
_____
_____
_____
_____
_____
_____
_____
_____

Day 6: Romans 2:4

* * *

Prayer for Today
God, today grant me
Strength to do as You please,
Wisdom to discern Your best for me,
Compassion to serve others who need You, and
Power to overcome the world's temptations.

BIBLE VERSE

Or do you presume on the riches of His kindness and
forbearance and patience, not knowing that God's
kindness is meant to lead you to repentance?
—Romans 2:4 (ESV)

REPENT

In this verse, we learn that God demonstrates His kindness to us for the purpose of bringing us to the decision to repent. Paul also mentions three of God's qualities: kindness, forbearance, and patience. Webster's defines *forbearance* as "refraining from the enforcement of something such as a debt, right or obligation." God is patient with me. He gives me time to realize that I need to repent, but I presume on His riches when I refuse.

It's important that Paul mentions these three traits of God in this verse. The Lord knows that I will make mistakes. He also realizes that I may not be fully aware of those mistakes, and as a result, He withholds the consequences of my actions. However, if I am spending time with Him in His Word, I will become aware of my shortcomings. At the time I become aware, He expects me to repent and turn from that behavior. If I do not immediately repent, I am presumptuous and taking advantage of His kindness, forbearance, and patience.

I often forget how deep His love is for me and that His deep desire is to see me repent, turn from my ways, and follow Him.

APPLICATION

I often forget that God is patient and kind. Forbearance is another form of patience. The debt I have to repay based on my sinful actions is overwhelming. But God, through His patience, has refrained from collecting on that debt. Rather, His Son Jesus paid that debt for me two thousand years before I was born.

This leads me to His kindness. He could enforce my debt upon me at any time, and I'd be condemned to a life of eternal punishment. Yet He gives me an opportunity to repent, turn from my evil ways, and follow Him.

All I am required to do is have enough courage to put my pride aside and repent.

COMMITMENT

By now, you realize that you've made mistakes throughout your life. The good news is that you will be forgiven, if you repent. The way Paul words this verse makes me realize just how patient God is with each of us. He is patient, but we should not procrastinate. We never know when our time will come. It is best to repent now. Then, you will be able to watch God work in your life in new and miraculous ways.

PRAYER

Lord, help me to focus today on true repentance, the only type of repentance that matters to You.

Journal

_____
_____
_____
_____
_____
_____
_____
_____
_____

Grateful

_____
_____
_____
_____
_____
_____
_____
_____
_____

Amends

_____
_____
_____
_____
_____
_____
_____
_____
_____

Day 7: 2 Corinthians 7:10

● ● ●

Prayer for Today
God, today grant me
Strength to do as You please,
Wisdom to discern Your best for me,
Compassion to serve others who need You, and
Power to overcome the world's temptations.

BIBLE VERSE

For godly grief produces repentance that leads to salvation
without regret, whereas worldly grief produces death.
—2 Corinthians 7:10 (ESV)

REPENT

We've all done or said something we wish we could take back, haven't
we? Fortunately, we have been given the gift of repentance. Repentance
is something we must each do periodically throughout our Christian life.
However, when we feel grief, it's not because we said or did something
good. One of the first things addicts who are beginning the long road to
recovery hear is that none of us got here because we were on a winning
streak. Quite the contrary; we are usually at an all-time low.

The fantastic news is that we are shown a way, by the eternal God,
to climb up out of the pit of grief and despair, right our wrongs, and
move forward. Grief is an emotion we feel when we know we have done
wrong. We may have wronged another person or disobeyed God. Our
disobedience is displeasing to Him. It hurts when we are disobedient;
it pain both us and our Lord, Who should be obeyed. Godly grief is
present when we have truly had enough and simply want to please Him.
But there are steps that must be taken; we must repent, and we must ask
for forgiveness. Godly grief and proper repentance lead to life and, most

importantly, salvation. The other type of grief is worldly grief, which produces pain, misery, and death.

APPLICATION

The critical difference between godly grief and worldly grief is the focus of our repentance. We need to be right with God and with others. True godly grief is focused on the actions that disrupted our relationships and the commitment we make to leave that element of life behind. Sometimes, we repent and ask God and others to forgive us. Other times, we need to be the one to forgive. We need to realize that there is a big difference between forgiving and forgetting. To forgive, we must confess our wrongdoing and commit to turning away from that act. To forget takes much more time and effort. Memories tend to take a long time to heal. They do not simply go away overnight. Be patient, be loving, be understanding, but most of all, foster a spirit of forgiving.

COMMITMENT

This is a great way to end the discussion on repentance. There is a huge difference between godly grief and worldly grief. The first leads to true repentance and salvation, without regret. The latter simply leads to death. Take the time and make the commitment to true godly repentance, and you'll begin to get past the regrets of previous bad decisions and actions.

PRAYER

Lord, help me to be filled with the godly grief that leads to repentance and life, and not the worldly grief that leads to death.

JOURNAL

_____
_____
_____
_____
_____
_____
_____
_____
_____

GRATEFUL

_____
_____
_____
_____
_____
_____
_____
_____
_____

AMENDS

_____
_____
_____
_____
_____
_____
_____
_____
_____

STEP 3 • • • • • • • • •

Faith

Faith   • • •

As I travelled deeper into my addiction, I lost the element of faith in my life. Faith is the ability to trust another person to do what I cannot do for myself. I trusted no one. Without trust and without faith, we are adrift in a very large world that has every kind of evil lurking around hidden corners waiting to attack. we are told that Satan is prowling around the earth, seeking to devour us.

When we choose to go at life alone, we take on Satan alone. That is not a fight we can win. Life continued to get more challenging and more difficult. The more difficult my life became, the more I depended on alcohol. And so began a downward spiral that tightened with every passing day.

I had inadvertently allowed Satan a foothold in my life. Alcohol became the toe in the door that Satan needed to divert me from the path God had planned for my life. Satan used my weakness to tell me that I was worth nothing. Every day, he told me I did not have what it takes to serve God.

Have you ever thought you were so far gone that God could never use you? That is Satan, exploiting your weakness to his benefit.

For a long time, I was angry with God and angry with myself. I was angry, in part, because I felt I could no longer be of use because of my sin and lack of faith. I bought into Satan's line: "Look how miserably weak and sinful you are. Do you really think God has a use for you?"

This week, we will work on restoring faith in the One Who can deliver us from the quagmire of addiction and restore us to a life of useful service.

The Mustard Seed   ● ● ●

Like the disciples, I did not understand why there were certain things I couldn't do. Eventually, I came to understand that my faith had wasted away to nothing. I didn't even have faith the size of a mustard seed. For my life to turn around, I realized that I needed to change my focus. I could no longer focus on me, the things that were wrong in my life, and the things that were wrong in the world. There was only one thing I could do: focus outside of myself, on Jesus. He is the one who will provide for all our needs. We have so much more than any other living things on this planet. Why do I allow myself to think that God doesn't care about me?

The solution to the hopelessness that comes from a lack of faith is to stop focusing on self and begin focusing on Jesus.

The Race   ● ● ●

In Hebrews 12: 1, Paul instructs us to live as though running a race. He also tells us that we must run with endurance. The race is never easy. We cannot have a strong finish at the end of a race if we spend our whole lives looking over our shoulder to see who is catching up. Likewise, we cannot finish strong if all we focus on are the mistakes we made throughout the race. The secret to finishing strong is to always be looking ahead. The best athletes know they must focus on the finish line; they cannot be distracted by what's happening around them or think about the mistakes they made along the way. Learn from our mistakes, yes. Be defined by them, no. God is an awesome God Who forgives us and enables us to use our flawed past for His future good. Why should I limit what God has planned to do with my life?

We are to be so focused on the finish line that we don't have time to reflect on what happened at the starting line.

Relationships   ● ● ●

Faith comes from growing in relationship with Jesus. I need to do everything in my power to protect my reputation, and more importantly,

I need to be full of the Spirit and faith. Faith grows from my relationship with God the Father and His Son, Jesus. My relationship with God grows when I spend time with Him in the Word and in prayer. By filling my time building a relationship with God and with His Son, I have no time for the sinful things of this world. When that happens, my reputation improves because people around me notice that my behavior is changing.

The road to faith begins by building a relationship with Jesus. There is not a better activity in this life on which to concentrate.

Finding Peace   ● ● ●

I cannot, or should not, rely on myself for the things I need to find peace. In Ephesians 2:8, Paul reminds me that my salvation came through nothing I did on my own, but rather through the gift of God and His grace. Is it any wonder, then, that when I find myself struggling and alone, I look back and find that those are the times I wandered furthest from God? It is not a coincidence. We are made and designed to follow Him, to accept His gift and His grace, and to be saved by faith in Him. When I find myself enveloped in fear and uncertainty, I need to run to Him, not from Him.

He will grant me the peace I seek if I first seek faith in Him.

Remove Doubt   ● ● ●

Have you allowed doubt to creep in and fill your life? Doubt is one of the enemy's greatest tools. He uses doubt to distract us from what God wants us to do and achieve. In Ephesians 6:13-20, Paul talks about the armor of God. One of the pieces of armor that God provides us is the shield of faith. A shield is large, and it protects the core of a warrior. I love the description Paul uses. He says that the shield of faith will protect us from the fiery darts of the evil one. I love that description because it paints such a clear picture of what Satan tries to do to us. Darts can inflict enough pain on their own. A fiery dart, on the other hand, can cause unimaginable pain if it connects with its target. God gives us the tools we need to fend off the attacks of Satan; we should use them to our full advantage.

We need to use faith as a shield to defend against the attacks of Satan.

Acceptance   ● ● ●

If God is willing to show me His favor and offer me the salvation that comes through faith, am I willing to accept that gift? That is a question we all need to ask daily. Am I willing to step out on faith and accept the gift He provides? Who among us would not accept a lavish gift from a friend? Not many of us would say no to a house or a car, or even enough money to get through to next payday so we can keep food on the table and a roof over our family's heads.

Yet the gift God offers is so much more. He offers us the opportunity to spend eternity with Him.

How can I say no to such a gift? All it takes is a willingness to step out on faith and say: yes, here I am.

God's Plan   ● ● ●

God has a plan for me. But until I learn to walk by faith and not by sight, I will never reach my full potential in Him. There is comfort in what I can see and experience. As we are told in verse 6, while we are at home in the body, we are away from the Lord. That is hard for me. I want to see and feel tangible proof that someone is with me. Yet, for a short period of time, while I am away from Him, He asks me to walk in faith.

The only way I can walk in faith is if I trust that His promises are true and that He will welcome me into eternity in His time.

Weekly Plan   ● ● ●

- Day 1: Matthew 17:20
- Day 2: Luke 7:50
- Day 3: Acts 6:5
- Day 4: Romans 5:1
- Day 5: 2 Corinthians 5:7
- Day 6: Ephesians 2:8
- Day 7: James 1:6

Day 1: Matthew 17:20

* * *

Prayer for Today
God, today grant me
Strength to do as You please,
Wisdom to discern Your best for me,
Compassion to serve others who need You, and
Power to overcome the world's temptations.

BIBLE VERSE

He said to them, "Because of your little faith. For truly, I say
to you, if you have faith like a grain of mustard seed, you
will say to this mountain, 'Move from here to there,' and it
will move, and nothing will be impossible for you."
—Matthew 17:20 (ESV)

FAITH

For several years, faith was a difficult concept for me to grasp. I tried to
live the way I thought God wanted me to, but something was missing. In
the world, I saw what I attributed to injustice and began to blame God.
I could not understand why things were going so badly in the world and
in my life, and this led me to feeling hopeless. I could not make anything
happen in my life. No matter how hard I tried, it seemed as though
everything was failing. I had lost my faith, and with it went my hope.
True, soul-deep hopelessness is the loneliest feeling imaginable, and that
is where I found myself.

I didn't realize it at the time, but the biggest problem I had in my life
was that I was trying to fix things. I was focused on me and not Jesus.

In today's verse, Jesus reminds me that I have not because I ask not. It is
said that the mustard seed is the smallest seed in the world. And Jesus tells
me that if my faith were even that big, I could ask Him to move mountains,

and He would do it. If my faith was only as large as the mustard seed, He promises me that nothing will be impossible. That statement should give each of us the hope we need to make our way through life. This one verse tells me that the only true limitation I face in life is having faith in the One Who paid the ultimate price for my life.

APPLICATION

Like the disciples, I didn't understand why there were certain things I could not do. Eventually, I came to understand that my faith had wasted away to nothing. I did not even have faith the size of a mustard seed. For my life to turn around, I needed to change my focus. I could no longer focus on me, the things that were wrong in my life, and the things that were wrong in the world. There was only one thing that I could do: focus outside of myself and focus on Jesus. He is the one who will provide for all our needs. We have so much more than any other living things on this planet. Why do I allow myself to think that God cannot possibly care about me?

The solution to the hopelessness that comes from a lack of faith is to stop focusing on self and begin focusing on Jesus.

COMMITMENT

True faith, in its smallest amount, can cause great change. In today's verse, Jesus says that we have not because we ask not. The reason we ask not is because our faith is so small. Look at the power Jesus describes, if all we have is the smallest amount of faith. Make a commitment today to open your heart and your mind to what Jesus has to teach you about true faith.

PRAYER

Lord, help me to live a life of faith today, a faith even the size of a mustard seed. Please provide me with the inner strength to then step out of the way and wait on You.

JOURNAL

_____
_____
_____
_____
_____
_____
_____
_____
_____

GRATEFUL

_____
_____
_____
_____
_____
_____
_____
_____
_____

AMENDS

_____
_____
_____
_____
_____
_____
_____
_____
_____

Day 2: Luke 7:50

* * *

Prayer for Today
God, today grant me
Strength to do as You please,
Wisdom to discern Your best for me,
Compassion to serve others who need You, and
Power to overcome the world's temptations.

BIBLE VERSE

And he said to the woman, "Your faith has saved you; go in peace."
—Luke 7:50 (ESV)

FAITH

Jesus shows us the value of true faith by His treatment of the sinful woman. Right before this verse, He declares that her sins are forgiven. He doesn't identify her sins, other than to say they are many. He declares her sins forgiven because of her faith. I think this is instructive for us.

There is nothing we can do to earn our forgiveness, but we must have faith to receive His gift.

I find it harder to forgive myself than Jesus finds it to forgive me. Satan's hook is to keep bringing me back to my past and reminding me that I can never be good enough. After all, when I remember who I was, it reminds why Jesus cannot use me. That is Satan's deception. When I struggle emotionally, it is usually because I allowed Satan to hook me and drag me back into my past.

APPLICATION

In Hebrews 12:1, Paul instructs us to live as though running a race. He also tells us that we must run with endurance. The race is never easy. We cannot have a strong finish at the end of a race if we spend our whole lives looking over our shoulder to see who is catching up. Likewise, we cannot finish strong if all we focus on are the mistakes we made throughout the race. The secret to finishing strong is to always be looking ahead. The best athletes know they must focus on the finish line; they cannot be distracted by what's happening around them or think about the mistakes they made along the way. Learn from our mistakes, yes. Be defined by them, no. God is an awesome God Who forgives us and enables us to use our flawed past for His future good. Why should I limit what God has planned to do with my life?

We are to be so focused on the finish line that we don't have time to reflect on what happened at the starting line.

COMMITMENT

I need to be so focused on what God has in store for me that I am not distracted by the traps Satan sets for me. Satan's classic trap is to have me looking over my shoulder, focusing on my past. God's release is to keep me focused on my future. This is such a short verse, but it is so powerful. Jesus simply says, "Your faith has saved you; go in peace." Once we learn to have faith in Him, we will begin to understand true peace.

PRAYER

Lord, help me to run each day as a race, focused on the finish line, on what You have in store for me, and on what You want to do through me.

JOURNAL

_____
_____
_____
_____
_____
_____
_____
_____
_____

GRATEFUL

_____
_____
_____
_____
_____
_____
_____
_____
_____

AMENDS

_____
_____
_____
_____
_____
_____
_____
_____
_____

Day 3: Acts 6:5

● ● ●

Prayer for Today
God, today grant me
Strength to do as You please,
Wisdom to discern Your best for me,
Compassion to serve others who need You, and
Power to overcome the world's temptations.

BIBLE VERSE

And what they said pleased the whole gathering, and they
chose Stephen, a man full of faith and of the Holy Spirit,
and Philip, and Prochorus, and Nicanor, and Timon, and
Parmenas, and Nicolaus, a proselyte of Antioch.
—Acts 6:5 ESV

FAITH

At first, this reading appears related to the topic of faith only because the word is mentioned in the verse. However, if we look back at Acts 6:1–4, we see what led up to this verse. They were in a period of time where the church was growing. They were gaining in number, and the ministry was being stretched. Many people needed help and were being served, and so there was a need to grow the number of those doing the ministry. The twelve disciples were focused on preaching the Word and prayer, but they needed others to meet the more basic needs of the congregation.

In response to the need, they decided to look for seven men to serve the ministry and work more directly with the parts of the congregation who needed personal assistance. They had three criteria by which they would select the additional seven disciples. The new disciples needed to be men with a good reputation, full of the Spirit, and full of wisdom. They appointed Stephen and six others to the positions. In addition to the three criteria by which they made their selection, Stephen was also described as a man full of faith.

APPLICATION

Faith comes from growing in relationship with Jesus. I need to do everything in my power to protect my reputation, and more importantly, I need to be full of the Spirit and faith. Faith grows from my relationship with God, the Father, and His Son, Jesus. My relationship with God grows when I spend time with Him in the Word and in prayer. By filling my time building a relationship with God and with His Son, I do not have time for the sinful things of this world. When that happens, my reputation improves because people around me notice that my behavior is changing.

The road to faith begins by building a relationship with Jesus. There is not a better activity in this life on which to concentrate.

COMMITMENT

Will you make a commitment to live a life of faith? You make this commitment by beginning to build a relationship with God the Father, His Son Jesus Christ, and the Holy Spirit. You build this relationship by spending time with Him in prayer, meditation, and reading of His Word. The only way you can hear God is to listen to His words. All you have to do is pick up your Bible and read. Your faith will grow as you learn what God is willing to do for you.

PRAYER

Lord, today give me the strength and resolve I need to build my relationship with You and forsake activities that are in conflict with my relationship with You.

JOURNAL

_____
_____
_____
_____
_____
_____
_____
_____
_____

GRATEFUL

_____
_____
_____
_____
_____
_____
_____
_____
_____

AMENDS

_____
_____
_____
_____
_____
_____
_____
_____
_____

Day 4: Romans 5:1

• • •

Prayer for Today
God, today grant me
Strength to do as You please,
Wisdom to discern Your best for me,
Compassion to serve others who need You, and
Power to overcome the world's temptations.

BIBLE VERSE

Therefore, since we have been justified by faith, we have
peace with God through our Lord Jesus Christ.
—Romans 5:1 (ESV)

FAITH

The best way to find peace is through faith in something greater than myself. Jesus is certainly greater than me. It is easy for me to look at the things I have done over the course of my life and think I have done great things, but how great have I really been? Not so much when compared with the Author and Perfecter of our faith. When I rely on the great things I've done, I ultimately find myself searching for peace. Any success I have in life is short-term and fleeting. What I long for is lasting, genuine, long-term peace: the feeling that anything I have done has made a difference. I do not get that from the temporal successes of this world. True peace comes from knowing that the things I have done will affect current and future generations.

That type of peace only comes through faith in the one Creator of the universe, through His Son, and through the Holy Spirit.

APPLICATION

I cannot, or should not, rely on myself for the things that I need to find peace. I cannot, or should not, rely on myself for the things I need to find peace. In Ephesians 2:8, Paul reminds me that my salvation came through nothing I did on my own, but rather through the gift of God and His grace. Is it any wonder, then, that when I find myself struggling and alone, I look back and find that those are the times I wandered furthest from God? It is not a coincidence. We are made and designed to follow Him, to accept His gift and His grace, and to be saved by faith in Him. When I find myself enveloped in fear and uncertainty, I need to run to Him, not from Him.

He will grant me the peace I seek if I first seek faith in Him.

COMMITMENT

As I seek peace today, will I also commit to a life of greater faith in the one true God? I need to realize that true peace doesn't come from the things I have done, but rather the things the Creator has done through me. We need to always run the race, looking ahead. God does not look at my past, so why should I? He has freed me from my past so that I might use my gifts and talents for the future benefit of others.

I must realize that true peace doesn't come from the things I have done, but rather the things the Creator has done through me.

PRAYER

God, help me live today by the faith You designed me to have.

JOURNAL

_____
_____
_____
_____
_____
_____
_____
_____
_____

GRATEFUL

_____
_____
_____
_____
_____
_____
_____
_____
_____

AMENDS

_____
_____
_____
_____
_____
_____
_____
_____
_____

Day 5: 2 Corinthians 5:6–7

• • •

Prayer for Today
God, today grant me
Strength to do as You please,
Wisdom to discern Your best for me,
Compassion to serve others who need You, and
Power to overcome the world's temptations.

BIBLE VERSE

So we are always of good courage. We know that while we are at home in
the body we are away from the Lord, for we walk by faith, not by sight.
—2 Corinthians 5:6-7 (ESV)

FAITH

Evidence of our faith is demonstrated by how we walk through life. Do I
walk by faith in God, or do I walk by what I see? Walking by sight is very
short-term and narrow. I can only see what is in front of me at that moment.
I cannot see even one second into the future. Jesus is the Author and Perfecter
of my faith. Why would I not follow Him? When I walk by sight, I allow
Satan to be my guide. Satan can use what I see to gradually lead me off
course. It is such a subtle drift. Paul warns us in Galatians 5:16 to walk by the
Spirit. This is the only way I can keep from gratifying the desires of the flesh.

Yet after many days of walking by sight, and when I look back to where
I was, only then do I realize how far off course I have been led by Satan.

APPLICATION

God has a plan for me. But until I learn to walk by faith and not by sight,
I will never reach my full potential in Him. There is comfort in what I can

see and experience. As we are told in verse 6, while we are at home in the body, we are away from the Lord. That is hard for me. I want to see and feel tangible proof that someone is with me. Yet, for a short period of time, while I am away from Him, He asks me to walk in faith.

The only way I can walk in faith is if I trust that His promises are true and that He will welcome me into eternity in His time.

COMMITMENT

Are you willing to make a commitment to walk by faith and not by sight? It sounds easy, and I suppose it gets easier the more we grow in our relationship with the Father. That said, there are always temptations to make decisions based on what we see. The challenge of faith is to bathe those decisions in prayer, ask God for His direction, and wait to see how He leads.

PRAYER

Lord, give me the strength to walk by faith in You today, not by the things I see. Help me to be found holy and pleasing to You by walking in faith.

Journal

_____
_____
_____
_____
_____
_____
_____
_____
_____

Grateful

_____
_____
_____
_____
_____
_____
_____
_____
_____

Amends

_____
_____
_____
_____
_____
_____
_____
_____
_____

Day 6: Ephesians 2:8

• • •

Prayer for Today
God, today grant me
Strength to do as You please,
Wisdom to discern Your best for me,
Compassion to serve others who need You, and
Power to overcome the world's temptations.

BIBLE VERSE

Ephesians 2:8 (ESV)
For by grace you have been saved through faith. And
this is not your own doing; it is the gift of God.
—Ephesians 2:8 (ESV)

FAITH

Our salvation comes through faith. That faith is given to us by grace. According to dictionary.com, one of the definitions of the word *grace* is "a manifestation of favor, especially by a superior." Our salvation, the forgiveness of our sins, is a direct result of God's favor. If a person in this world shows us favor, we typically say thank you. When I was at my lowest point, God offered me His grace. He offers me His grace daily. He forgave me for my sin and continues to do so.

APPLICATION

If God is willing to show me His favor and offer me the salvation that comes through faith, am I willing to accept that gift? That is a question we all need to ask daily. Am I willing to step out on faith and accept the gift He provides? Who among us would not accept a lavish gift from a friend?

Not many of us would say no to a house or a car, or even enough money to get through to next payday so we can keep food on the table and a roof over our family's heads.

Yet the gift God offers is so much more. He offers us the opportunity to spend eternity with Him.

How can I say no to such a gift? All it takes is a willingness to step out on faith and say, "Yes, here I am."

COMMITMENT

God has provided you with the tremendous gift of faith. We are saved by the grace that comes through faith. We have done nothing to deserve or earn the salvation God provides us through His Son. Take time today to reflect on God's grace. Take the time to thank Him for the faith that comes through His gift of grace.

PRAYER

Thank You, Lord, for the gift of salvation that comes only through faith, not through anything I have done to earn that gift.

Day 7: James 1:6

● ● ●

Prayer for Today
God, today grant me
Strength to do as You please,
Wisdom to discern Your best for me,
Compassion to serve others who need You, and
Power to overcome the world's temptations.

BIBLE VERSE

But let him ask in faith, with no doubting, for the one who doubts
is like a wave of the sea that is driven and tossed by the wind.
—James 1:6 (ESV)

FAITH

When we pray, we are required to ask in faith. Look at how the one who
doubts is described. That person is likened to a wave in the sea that is
tossed around by the wind. Have you ever been to the ocean and looked
at the waves? They are constantly churning. Did you see what those waves
do to the sand beneath them? The more wind, the more churning of the
water. The sand beneath those waves is churned up, and it causes the water
to be cloudy. If there is enough wind, the churning can be so strong that
it causes a sense of unease. When doubt enters life, there is an unsettled
feeling about everything we do. Do not allow doubt to enter your life.
Make your requests for God's direction, having faith that He will answer
according to His will.

Doubt leads to confusion and a loss of direction. Faith removes the
doubt, allows the water to clear, and restores a sense of purpose and
direction.

Application

Have you allowed doubt to creep in and fill your life? Doubt is one of the enemy's greatest tools. He uses doubt to distract us from what God wants us to do and achieve. In Ephesians 6:13–20, Paul tells us to put on the whole armor of God. One of the pieces of armor God provides is the shield of faith. A shield is large, and it protects the core of a warrior. I love the description Paul uses. You must take up the shield of faith and deflect doubt.

The shield of faith protects us from the fiery darts of the evil one. I love that description because it paints such a clear picture of what Satan tries to do to us. Darts can inflict enough pain on their own. A fiery dart, on the other hand, can cause unimaginable pain if it connects with its target. God gives us the tools we need to fend off the attacks of Satan; we should use them to our full advantage.

We need to use faith as a shield to defend against the attacks of Satan.

Commitment

Faith is a defensive weapon we use to defend against the doubt that Satan tries to sow. Today, commit to using the shield of faith to put distance between you and Satan. Use the shield of faith that God provides to draw closer to Him.

Prayer

Lord, give me the strength to pick up the shield of faith today and use it to draw nearer to You.

JOURNAL

_____
_____
_____
_____
_____
_____
_____
_____
_____

GRATEFUL

_____
_____
_____
_____
_____
_____
_____
_____
_____

AMENDS

_____
_____
_____
_____
_____
_____
_____
_____
_____

STEP 4 •••••••••

God's Armor

God's Provision ●●●

God provides His armor to believers so they will stand when attacked by Satan. Satan is a fierce opponent. He lurks around corners but sometimes hides in plain sight. In Ephesians 6:10–17, Paul tells us that God provides us with the armor we need to stand firm when challenges come our way.

Paul tells us to be strong in the Lord and in the strength of His might. We do not have the strength, on our own, to take a stand against Satan and win. If we try to fight the battle on our own, we will lose. God knows that, and Paul reminds us we need God's strength to overcome. Paul also tells us to put on the whole armor of God. The Lord provides us with a complete set of armor to defend against the attacks of Satan. These attacks are described by Paul as fiery darts.

Notice that all but one item of armor is to be used for defensive purposes. The only offensive weapon we are provided is the sword of truth, which is the Word of God. God's armor is designed to protect all our vital organs from spiritual injury. We must put on the full armor of God to successfully stand against the enemy.

Resist Satan ●●●

Paul tells us to resist Satan because his attacks are often unexpected. Satan will attack when we are weak and vulnerable. He loves it when we are down. When we are down, he kicks us that much harder. The phrase "resist Satan, and he will flee from you" sounds easy enough. However, when we choose to resist Satan, we can be in for the fight of a lifetime. Satan does not go away easily. Sometimes, his assault is a full-on attack. Many times, I find that he picks away at the areas where I am weakest. His constant picking away can wear on us if we are not on full alert.

John MacArthur's devotional entitled *Resisting the Devil* says, "Spiritual warfare isn't as much a frontal attack on Satan's domain as it is the ability to resist his advances." Satan is sneaky and subtle. He is direct and hits us head-on. We have the tools we need to withstand Satan's attacks if we put on God's armor daily. It does us no good to attack Satan head-on. He will win that fight every time. He is too strong for us if we try to take him on directly. That's why God's armor is made up of so many defensive weapons.

Put on God's Armor

When we put on God's armor, we can resist Satan. Like a warrior headed to battle, we are told to put on each piece of armor every day. It does no good to go into battle with only part of the armor in place. Leaving even one piece behind is like putting none of it on. God's armor is a system of defense. The pieces of armor are less effective unless we use them all. The armor of a Roman warrior was designed to work as a defensive system. When all pieces of the armor were worn together, the warrior was completely protected.

There is one offensive weapon in the armor that God provides. The other pieces of armor are defensive. The "sword of the Spirit, which is the Word of God" is the only piece of armor that He provides for offense. God gives us His Word to use on offense. Satan twists God's words for his benefit. When we know God's Word, we recognize Satan's deceit. Satan is crafty and twists God's words, giving them meaning He never intended. In Matthew 4, Satan tested Jesus by twisting God's words. Because Jesus knew God's words, He was able to resist Satan.

Go Forward and Resist ● ● ●

We have God's armor; now it is time to put it into action. Each day we must put on God's armor: the belt of truth, the breastplate of righteousness, the shoes of the Gospel of peace, the shield of faith, the helmet of salvation, and the sword of the Spirit. Satan will attack; there is no question. The only question is, will I be ready when the attack comes?

I began to stumble into addiction when I did not put on the armor of God. The struggle began with my faith, and rather than push through it, I drifted away. I put God's armor in the closet. I did not think I needed His armor. I was convinced I could fight the fight on my own. The only thing I accomplished was to walk on the battlefield and wait for the death blow. Take time to really study God's armor and decide to wear it every single day.

Weekly Plan ● ● ●

- Day 1: Ephesians 6:13
- Day 2: Ephesians 6:14a
- Day 3: Ephesians 6:14b
- Day 4: Ephesians 6:15
- Day 5: Ephesians 6:16
- Day 6: Ephesians 6:17
- Day 7: Ephesians 6:10–11

Day 1: Ephesians 6:13

● ● ●

Prayer for Today
God, today grant me
Strength to do as You please,
Wisdom to discern Your best for me,
Compassion to serve others who need You, and
Power to overcome the world's temptations.

BIBLE VERSE

Therefore take up the whole armor of God, that you may be able
to withstand in the evil day, and having done all, to stand firm.
—Ephesians 6:13

GOD'S ARMOR

Have you thought about what it means to take up the whole armor of God?
Before a warrior goes into battle, he puts on all his armor. He puts on this
armor so he is protected in battle. Each day is a battle. We usually have
no idea where an attack will come from, but we know we will encounter
situations that trip us up and challenge our faith or our sobriety, or both.
God knows that and has provided each of us with the tools we need to
succeed each day. God offers us His armor. We must take up the whole
armor of God so we can stand firm. If we only put on part of His armor,
we remain exposed and give evil a chance to attack.

We must take up the whole armor of God so we can stand firm.

APPLICATION

Throughout this week, we will look at each piece of armor described in the
text. There are six pieces of armor, and all of them are defensive, except

one. If you follow sports, you have probably heard that the best offense is a strong defense. That holds true for the Christian walk and the walk of sobriety. Each day brings new challenges. Early sobriety is challenging. Strong temptations face us each and every day. The only way we can get through is to rely on God. We have proven that we cannot defeat addiction on our own. We need help from a power greater than ourselves. That power is God. He gives us what we need to succeed.

We need to be diligent daily, accept what God offers, prepare each morning, and determine to use what He provides to defend against the attacks that will come.

COMMITMENT

Each morning, I will commit to prayer at the beginning of my day. I will make conscious note of each piece of God's armor and ask Him for the strength to get through the day and stand firm.

PRAYER

Lord, help me to be aware today of each piece of armor You provide me. Help me to put on that armor and use it to defend against the attacks of Satan. Help me to stand firm so You may be of service to others through me.

JOURNAL

_____
_____
_____
_____
_____
_____
_____
_____
_____
_____

GRATEFUL

_____
_____
_____
_____
_____
_____
_____
_____
_____
_____

AMENDS

_____
_____
_____
_____
_____
_____
_____
_____
_____
_____

Day 2: Ephesians 6:14a

* * *

Prayer for Today
God, today grant me
Strength to do as You please,
Wisdom to discern Your best for me,
Compassion to serve others who need You, and
Power to overcome the world's temptations.

BIBLE VERSE

Stand therefore, having fastened on the belt of truth.
—Ephesians 6:14a

GOD'S ARMOR

In the first part of this verse, Paul is telling believers to begin putting on their armor. As you recall from Ephesians 6:13, Paul instructs us to put on the whole armor of God. And why does he tell us that? So we can stand firm in the evil day. There are temptations all around us. Satan is constantly attacking us. Sometimes, it is a full-on assault; other times, he picks away at the edges. Satan and his fallen angels understand God's Word and will use it to lead us astray, one small step at a time. Look at Matthew 4:11. This section talks about Jesus being led into the wilderness to be tempted by Satan. In these verses, Satan uses Bible verses to tempt Jesus. What saved Jesus from these temptations was a firm understanding of God's Word. Jesus was able to see through the misleading of Satan and remain faithful to His Father.

And why does he tell us to put on the whole armor of God? So we can stand firm in the evil day.

APPLICATION

I believe it is instructive that Paul tells us to put on the belt of truth first. The belt holds everything together. Without the belt, the whole armor of

God falls apart. The belt of truth is our first line of defense against the attacks of Satan and his fallen angels. We must have a firm understanding of God's Word if we are to defend against evil attacks. We should be careful when looking into God's Word for direction. It is easy to take one verse by itself and think we understand it. When we investigate God's Word, individual verses are important, but we must also look to the verses around them to understand the context of the verse. Understanding the context of the verse and how it weaves into the fabric of scripture is what gives us the ability to root out false interpretation and misguided instruction.

The belt of truth is our first line of defense against the attacks of Satan and his fallen angels.

COMMITMENT

Commit yourself, today, to spending time with God in His Word. His Word will provide you with comfort and direction. No matter what situation you're facing, God has seen them all. He will help you. In Ecclesiastes 1:9, we are told that there is nothing new under the sun. Finally, in 1 Corinthians 10:13, Paul tells us that there is no temptation that is not common to man. But he does not leave it there. He takes it a step further and reminds us that God will never allow us to be tempted beyond what we can bear. With the temptation, He will provide a way of escape so we can endure. What a great promise.

The Christian walk is not a sprint; it is a marathon. Marathons require tremendous endurance. Today, are you willing to train spiritually for the spiritual marathon that lays ahead?

PRAYER

Lord, help me to gain a deeper understanding of Your Word. Lead me today to the verses that will minister to my needs. Help me to put on the belt of truth so I may bear up under whatever comes my way today.

Journal

_____
_____
_____
_____
_____
_____
_____
_____
_____

Grateful

_____
_____
_____
_____
_____
_____
_____
_____
_____

Amends

_____
_____
_____
_____
_____
_____
_____
_____
_____

Day 3: Ephesians 6:14b

● ● ●

Prayer for Today
God, today grant me
Strength to do as You please,
Wisdom to discern Your best for me,
Compassion to serve others who need You, and
Power to overcome the world's temptations.

BIBLE VERSE

And having put on the breastplate of righteousness.
—Ephesians 6:14b

GOD'S ARMOR

The second piece of armor Paul mentions is the breastplate of righteousness. Think about the function of the breastplate. The breastplate takes the brunt of a full-on frontal attack. It was the Roman equivalent of today's Kevlar vest. The breastplate protects a warrior's vital organs. In a frontal attack, it is the last line of defense. When everything else fails, warriors rely on their breastplate for protection.

Among other organs, the breastplate will protect your heart against the attack of Satan.

APPLICATION

Look at what Luke has to say about the heart:

The good person out of the good treasure of his heart produces
good, and the evil person out of his evil treasure produces evil,
for out of the abundance of the heart his mouth speaks.
—Luke 6:45 (ESV)

And look at Peter's comments to Ananias in Acts:

> But Peter said, "Ananias, why has Satan filled your heart to lie to the Holy Spirit and to keep back for yourself part of the proceeds of the land? ⁴ While it remained unsold, did it not remain your own? And after it was sold, was it not at your disposal? Why is it that you have contrived this deed in your heart? You have not lied to man but to God."
> —Acts 5:3–4 (ESV)

Is it any wonder that the second piece of the armor of God is the breastplate of righteousness? From the beginning of time every intention of man's heart has been evil continually (see Genesis 6:5). We must guard our heart closely. If we let our guard down, even if only for a split second, Satan will pounce. Just look at what happened in Acts 5 with Ananias and Saphira. They let their guard down, Satan convinced them to lie about the amount of money they made from the sale of their ground. As a result of their lie, God struck them dead.

If we are not careful to protect our heart, it can quickly become Satan's playground.

Commitment

We must take matters of the heart very seriously. Make a commitment today to ask God to show you how to put on the breastplate of righteousness. Ask Him to guard your heart against the attacks of Satan.

Do not allow Satan to get a firm grip on your heart, it can have deadly consequences.

Prayer

Lord, thank You for the armor of God, and for the breastplate that protects my heart from the attacks of Satan. Help me stand firm behind Your breastplate today.

JOURNAL

_____
_____
_____
_____
_____
_____
_____
_____
_____

GRATEFUL

_____
_____
_____
_____
_____
_____
_____
_____
_____

AMENDS

_____
_____
_____
_____
_____
_____
_____
_____
_____

Day 4: Ephesians 6:15

* * *

Prayer for Today
God, today grant me
Strength to do as You please,
Wisdom to discern Your best for me,
Compassion to serve others who need You, and
Power to overcome the world's temptations.

Bible Verse

And, as shoes for your feet, having put on the
readiness given by the gospel of peace.
—Ephesians 6:15

God's Armor

Today, we will look at the third piece of the armor of God: the shoes for your feet. It is said that the Roman soldiers wore boots in combat that had nails in the bottom, almost like the cleats worn by today's football players. The purpose of these boots, or shoes, was to help keep the warrior's feet firmly planted during battle. Without these boots, soldiers ran the risk of slipping during battle. The battles these soldiers faced were fierce and brutal. It was almost all hand-to-hand combat. Any slip on the part of a soldier in those days was almost certainly a death warrant. The boots kept the warrior's feet firmly planted in the battle; with them, he was able to keep his balance and stand his ground and defend against the enemy. The only difference between what the Roman warriors faced then and what we as believers face today is that they could see their enemy. We oftentimes cannot see our enemy, but we most certainly can feel his presence.

The boots kept the warrior's feet firmly planted in the battle; with them, he was able to keep his balance and stand his ground and defend against the enemy.

APPLICATION

So God has given us boots to use in the battles we face. Our boots, however, are a little bit different. Look at how Paul defines the boots that are part of our holy armor of God. In the ESV, the word is translated "shoes," but the point is still the same. The Gospel of peace is what we are to wear as shoes. The Gospel of peace will prepare us for when the battle comes. We do not have to go find the fight; Satan is skilled at bringing the fight to God's people. Just like the Roman soldier, the only chance we have to win the fight is to be prepared and stand our ground. To be strong in the Lord, as Paul says in verse 10, we must have a firm understanding of God's Gospel. We need to know the Gospel of Jesus, not the gospel of the guy next door or a preacher on the most recent podcast. God has put a lot of tools at our disposal. Everything we need is found in His Word. Resources like scholarly commentaries are great when we struggle to understand the meaning of a passage, but we must keep God's Word as the primary source of wisdom.

God has put a lot of tools at our disposal. All the tools we need are found in His Word.

COMMITMENT

Will you make a commitment today to understanding the Gospel of peace? The Gospel of peace that Jesus offers will keep us firmly grounded when attacks come our way. It is not a matter of if; it's a matter of when we will face attack. Again, the best offense is a great defense, and the Gospel of Jesus will prepare us for the attacks that will inevitably come our way.

PRAYER

Lord, today, help me understand Your Gospel. In these verses, You refer to Your Word as the Gospel of peace. Grant me the peace I need today to face whatever Satan throws my way.

Journal

_____
_____
_____
_____
_____
_____
_____
_____
_____

Grateful

_____
_____
_____
_____
_____
_____
_____
_____
_____

Amends

_____
_____
_____
_____
_____
_____
_____
_____
_____

Day 5: Ephesians 6:16

● ● ●

Prayer for Today
God, today grant me
Strength to do as You please,
Wisdom to discern Your best for me,
Compassion to serve others who need You, and
Power to overcome the world's temptations.

BIBLE VERSE

In all circumstances take up the shield of faith, with which
you can extinguish all the flaming darts of the evil one.
—Ephesians 6:16 (ESV)

GOD'S ARMOR

As you grow in your walk with Christ, your faith will be tested. The next
piece of armor God provides us is His shield of faith. I like the image of a
shield. It is a large piece of armor typically worn on the arm of a warrior.
All the other pieces of armor are physically attached to the body to protect
a specific body part. The shield, by comparison, while physically attached
to the arm, may be moved to defend any unprotected area. The shield, for
a Roman warrior, was the very first line of physical defense. The same is
true of our faith. We never know precisely where Satan will attack. What
we do know is that he seeks out areas where we are spiritually the weakest.
Just like the shield of the Roman warrior is broad and strong, so must our
faith be broad and strong.

We never know precisely where Satan will attack. What we do know
is that he seeks out areas where we are the weakest.

APPLICATION

If we are going to have any success in our battle against the personal attacks of Satan, we must make sure that our shield of faith is both broad and strong. Our spiritual shield is the primary defense we have against the attacks of Satan. Look at how Paul describes the attacks of Satan. I can only imagine how difficult it is to fend off incoming darts or spears. Imagine what it would be like if those darts were also covered in flame. The imagery is terrifying.

I can only imagine how difficult it is to fend off incoming darts or spears. Imagine what it would be like if those darts were also covered in flame.

COMMITMENT

We must make a commitment to seek a closer relationship with God the Father every day. We can only do that through His Son Jesus. As our relationship grows deeper, we become more firmly rooted. As we become more firmly rooted, our faith grows. As our faith grows, our shield increases in size and strength. The closer we grow to God, the harder Satan will attack. We need a broad and strong shield of faith to survive those attacks.

PRAYER

Lord, help me to draw closer to You today and have a deeper relationship with You. Lord, cause my faith to grow so my shield is strong enough to survive those attacks.

JOURNAL

_____
_____
_____
_____
_____
_____
_____
_____
_____

GRATEFUL

_____
_____
_____
_____
_____
_____
_____
_____
_____

AMENDS

_____
_____
_____
_____
_____
_____
_____
_____
_____

Day 6: Ephesians 6:17

• • •

Prayer for Today
God, today grant me
Strength to do as You please,
Wisdom to discern Your best for me,
Compassion to serve others who need You, and
Power to overcome the world's temptations.

Bible Verse

And take the helmet of salvation, and the sword
of the Spirit, which is the word of God.
—Ephesians 6:17 (ESV)

God's Armor

We have reached the last two pieces of armor that God provides for our use. The last piece of defensive armor He offers is the helmet of salvation. This is important because the helmet protects the head, and ultimately the mind, of the warrior. Satan loves to attack us, and one of the easiest points of attack for him is to go after our mind. In our mind, Satan can plant seeds of doubt. He can cause us to doubt our faith. And he can cause us to question whether God can even use us at all. We cannot allow Satan that type of access to our mind. The final piece of God's armor is the sword of the Spirit. This sword is the Word of God. We can only do battle with Satan if we are firmly grounded in God's Word. We must know His Word and use it so we are solidly grounded in faith. God's Word is the only way we can push Satan back.

APPLICATION

In my walk with Jesus, I am constantly reminded that I am firm in the salvation He offers. This helmet of salvation allows me to get through each day. I can rest knowing that no matter what the world throws at me today, God has rescued me. He has provided me with salvation. He has paid the price. I am grateful for that salvation. As a result, I want to be closer to Him. I want to understand what He wants for me. Most of all, I want to be able to beat back the attacks of Satan. The best thing I can do for myself each day is to pick up the sword of the Spirit, God's Word, and get to know Him. I must allow Him to teach me what He wants me to know and allow Him to fight my battles for me. The only way I can achieve that goal is to know His Word and allow that Word to work in my life.

COMMITMENT

Are you ready to get to know Jesus on a deeper level? Commit today to putting on the last piece of defensive armor, the helmet of salvation. Take comfort in the fact that no matter how bad things may seem today, there is a tomorrow, and there is an eternity. God offers you the helmet of salvation to provide you with the confidence and peace you need to get through the day. For all this armor to work, we must take up the one offensive weapon He provides: the sword of the Spirit. The armor works when we know His Word and truly understand what it says. Then you will be equipped to do battle with Satan.

PRAYER

Lord, help me put on the helmet of salvation and pick up the sword of the Spirit today. Help me to draw closer to You through Your Word. Help me to fight back Satan with the truth of Your Word. Grant me victory today.

Journal

_____
_____
_____
_____
_____
_____
_____
_____

Grateful

_____
_____
_____
_____
_____
_____
_____
_____

Amends

_____
_____
_____
_____
_____
_____
_____
_____

Day 7: Ephesians 6:10–11

● ● ●

Prayer for Today

God, today grant me

Strength to do as You please,

Wisdom to discern Your best for me,

Compassion to serve others who need You, and

Power to overcome the world's temptations.

BIBLE VERSE

> Finally, be strong in the Lord and in the strength of his
> might. Put on the whole armor of God, that you may
> be able to stand against the schemes of the devil.
> —Ephesians 6:10–11 (ESV)

GOD'S ARMOR

I think it is fitting to end the section on God's armor where Paul began. Paul instructs us to do two things: first, be strong, and second, put on the whole armor. God provides us with the tools we need, but we must act. Preparing for battle requires strength. God provides us with the strength we need in His Son. That is a tremendous burden lifted. Satan schemes continually. He looks for weak spots in our armor and creates clever schemes to take advantage of those weak spots. A warrior's armor is effective only when the whole armor is put on correctly. A warrior who leaves a piece of armor behind is open to attack. We must use the armor we have been given correctly. Then we will be able to stand in battle. Also, remember that all but one of the pieces of armor is for defensive purposes. We don't need to look for a fight; it will find us. Do not forget the power of the one offensive weapon He provides us. The sword of the spirit, which is the Word of God, will keep us grounded in battle.

APPLICATION

Each morning, we need to consciously inventory the armor we have been provided. Before our day starts, we must put on each and every piece of armor. Once the day begins, the attacks are likely to come. Spiritual warfare is quick and intense. When an attack comes, we won't have time to go back home and grab our armor. The armor must be on and in position to be effective in our daily battles with Satan. Never let your guard down. The moment your guard is lowered, Satan is bound to attack. We must always be prepared and stay focused and allow God to fight our battles for us.

COMMITMENT

Make a genuine commitment today to trust God for His strength and His might. He wants to see us succeed. He wants us to ask Him for help. When we ask Him for help, He answers. We cannot do life on our own. I should know. I tried and failed miserably. My life is so much better when I trust Him for everything that happens every day. Begin your day by thanking Him for all He has provided you. You are blessed more than you may realize.

PRAYER

Lord, thank You for the armor You provide. Your armor and Your strength give me what I need to get through each day. Help me as I learn to lean on You more each day.

JOURNAL

_____
_____
_____
_____
_____
_____
_____
_____
_____

GRATEFUL

_____
_____
_____
_____
_____
_____
_____
_____
_____

AMENDS

_____
_____
_____
_____
_____
_____
_____
_____
_____

STEP 5 •••••••••

Seek Shelter

Life Is a Team Sport ● ● ●

Most who struggle with addiction forget that life is a team sport. As their addiction deepens, they turn inward. There are many reasons for that, but at the exact time they should be looking for support from others, they turn inward. In this section, we will look at the necessity of seeking shelter. One of the ways life can jump off the tracks happens when we choose to battle life, head-on, on our own. Life is not meant to be lived in a vacuum. It's a team sport. We need to learn to work together as friends, family, and community. To work together effectively, we need to understand that each person is individually gifted and therefore qualified to participate in groups outside of self. The Christian community works much better when we combine our talents and work together toward a common purpose: furthering God's message to those who are lost and struggling.

Soul-Deep Salvation ● ● ●

Probably the greatest truth in all that David writes is the fact that his love for God is soul-deep. David does not just seek God when times are tough; he blesses God in all situations. David spends a lot of time in self-evaluation and introspection. Any time David asks God for help, he typically starts by asking the Lord to judge his heart and his motivations and his actions. Before anything else, David wants to be found to be right before God.

Does he make mistakes? Yes. Are they big mistakes? Sometimes. But his mistakes grieve him deeply, not because he has been caught, but because he has violated God's direction for his life.

God's impact on David's life was complete. His impact was through and through. David was even referred to as a man after God's own heart. I'm not trying to justify my actions or excuse the bad decisions I make, but David made mistakes. Some of them were huge. God dealt with David and punished him. But David never lost his standing with the Lord. God never abandoned him. Likewise, if we are truly repentant of our sins, God will not abandon us, either. He may punish us, but that is out of His love for us. If we are corrected, and if we allow ourselves to learn from the correction, we will be much better Christians for the process.

Be Comforted ● ● ●

Paul says in 2 Corinthians 1:4 (ESV), "Who comforts us in all our affliction, so that we may be able to comfort those who are in any affliction, with the comfort with which we ourselves are comforted by God." In my mind, I can hear the voice of J. Vernon McGhee, saying, "Now friend, God does not promise you an easy life." Our suffering is for a purpose, so that we can comfort those with the comfort God provides to us. Throughout life, we face many challenges and hardships. God never promised us an easy life. He only promises a fulfilling life when we follow His commands and precepts. The Lord does not prepare us for a life of solitude; He prepares us for a life that pleases Him, benefits others, and shines light on His goodness (Matthew 5:16). We are shine our light in a way that impacts those around us and points them to His glory.

Times of Trial ● ● ●

We will go through trials of many kinds (James 1:2). For me, I made a series of bad decisions that led me to become addicted to alcohol. It was a very dark and miserable time in my life. I made everyone around me miserable. I spent a lot of time trying to figure out why God allowed me to go through that hardship. I lost my ability to speak publicly. My self-confidence was shot. Before I became addicted to alcohol, I taught Sunday school and wrote Bible studies. After I got out of rehab, I could not utter a complete sentence in public without having a full-blown panic attack. I remember a Bible study I was trying to lead. The words were in my head; I simply could not get them to come out of my mouth. I eventually closed my materials and told the group they should continue without me.

I still have a hard time speaking in public, although it has gotten better. But you know what? I learned that not only can I write, but I enjoy writing. Because of the internet, our world has become so much smaller. I can write something today that goes all around the world.

Seek Shelter ● ● ●

When times of trial and trouble come, we are told to seek shelter, first in Him. When we do that, He takes care of us. He provides us with shelter and protection against the storms of life. In this section, we look at David's reaction to the difficulties of life, as expressed in the book of Psalms. David was identified by God as a man after His own heart. Yet David still had his struggles and his failings. But when you look at his life, you'll see that he was a man who trusted God for his daily protection and provision.

David was a fierce warrior. He was pursued by the king's army. He would have been put to death if caught. Clearly, he was not perfect. But as you will see in this small selection of verses, he relied fully on God. He did not turn to God only in times of trouble. He also praised God when times were good. He took time to thank God for His protection and His direction. He took time to offer God the honor that He so richly deserves. David was grateful and thankful to God. I believe that is a big part of the reason why God answered him in the tough times. David had a relationship with God. His communication with God was two way, not one way.

God's Shield

Throughout these verses, you will see that David refers frequently to God's shield. God provides us with His shield for protection. In David's life, he needed physical protection because he was frequently pursued. There were many who wanted to see him dead. While that may be true for us today, we usually face spiritual attacks. You can at least see a physical attack coming, unlike spiritual attacks, which take many forms. Spiritual attacks are often played out in our mind. Difficult situations arise, and we must make a decision. How will we respond to whatever the difficulty might be? We often know what the right decision is, but we make a bad choice because it's easier. God knows that our decisions will be difficult; that's why He provides us with His shield. He protects us during those difficult times.

Rock, Stronghold, Refuge, Fortress

David uses many different terms to describe God. These four are my favorites. God will be our rock. He is solid and can be trusted in any and every situation. He will not move. When Satan attacks, we can trust that God will be there and be solid. Because God is a solid rock, He is also a stronghold for us. We can hang on to Him. Sometimes, it feels like we are barely hanging on by our fingertips. That's okay. No matter how hard the wind blows, He will not move. We just need to tighten our grip. Finally, David calls God a fortress. I think of an ancient castle when I think of a fortress. These fortresses are well fortified. They are typically made of stone or similar material. Their walls reach high and provide a place of concealment for those on the inside who are defending against potential invaders. God is that fortress for us.

Relationship

David was able to experience God in this way because he had a relationship with God. He developed a relationship with God in the good times and the bad. His love for God was soul-deep, from deep within. He sought God's direction throughout his life. God asked him to do some difficult things, but he trusted God, and in most cases did as God directed. We must develop a relationship with Him if we want to be fully protected by Him.

Weekly Plan

- Day 1: Psalm 3:3
- Day 2: Psalm 7:10
- Day 3: Psalm 18:2
- Day 4: Psalm 18:30
- Day 5: Psalm 18:35
- Day 6: Psalm 28:7
- Day 7: Psalm 33:20

Day 1: Psalm 3:3

• • •

Prayer for Today
God, today grant me
Strength to do as You please,
Wisdom to discern Your best for me,
Compassion to serve others who need You, and
Power to overcome the world's temptations.

BIBLE VERSE

But you, O Lord, are a shield about me, my
glory, and the lifter of my head.
—Psalm 3:3 (ESV)

SEEK SHELTER

We must all seek shelter from time to time. The question is, where will we seek that shelter? We have seen that God cares deeply for us. He knows everything about us. He understands what we are going through: our struggles, sadness, emptiness, and loneliness. God also knows when we are happy and excited. He knows these things before even we realize them. That said, God wants us to trust Him. We are to run to Him in good times and bad. Our first choice, no matter what problem or happiness we are facing, should always be to run to Him first. He wants to be our first line of defense, and He wants to be the One we run to when we need shelter.

APPLICATION

In this verse, David lists three of God's characteristics. He is my shield, our glory, and the One Who lifts my head. God wants to be my shield. He wants to protect me from the dangers that lurk around dark corners.

When I am in trouble, He will be my shield to fend off the attacks of the evil one. God is also my glory. His presence and goodness cannot be measured. When I think of glory, I think of bright sunshine and cloudless blue skies. Even when things are swirling around me and there feels like there's no way out, I am reminded that He is our glory. There is a better place waiting for us, if we will just trust Him. Finally, He is the lifter of my head. There are days when I feel like I can't get out of bed, much less go to work or do the things I need to do. If I am willing to trust Him, He will give me the strength to carry on.

COMMITMENT

God wants to do so much for us. He wants to be there for us. We are protected, but we must take the first step. If there is a tornado headed your way, the storm shelter cannot protect you unless you run to it, open the door, and walk in. God is our storm shelter, but we must take the first step toward Him if we want to experience His protection from the storms of life.

PRAYER

Lord, help me today to begin taking steps toward You. I don't want You to be my last line of defense. Rather, I want You to be my first line of defense. Help me to step toward You today.

JOURNAL

_____
_____
_____
_____
_____
_____
_____
_____
_____

GRATEFUL

_____
_____
_____
_____
_____
_____
_____
_____
_____

AMENDS

_____
_____
_____
_____
_____
_____
_____
_____
_____

Day 2: Psalm 7:10

● ● ●

Prayer for Today
God, today grant me
Strength to do as You please,
Wisdom to discern Your best for me,
Compassion to serve others who need You, and
Power to overcome the world's temptations.

BIBLE VERSE

My shield is with God, who saves the upright in heart.
—Psalm 7:10 (ESV)

SEEK SHELTER

In Psalm 7, David is talking about taking refuge in God. In the first two verses of the chapter, it is clear that David's enemies are pursuing him, seeking to tear him apart like a lion. He even describes having his soul torn apart into pieces. While I cannot relate to David's exact situation, I can imagine that he felt abject terror of being caught by his pursuers. They did not just want him dead; they wanted him completely and utterly destroyed. I have never been pursued like this by anyone. Yet God called David was a man after His own heart. David was doing what God wanted him to do, and still people were seeking to destroy him in an extremely violent manner. Even though he is being pursued by his enemies, he clearly states in verse 1 that he is seeking refuge with God.

APPLICATION

As I think about how this applies to my life, I look at verse 10. David describes God as his shield and as the One Who saves the upright in heart.

David's heart was right with God. Because his heart was right with God, he knew that the Lord would protect him. I think about how a lion attacks, pouncing and mauling his prey. In the face of violent attack, David knows that he needs a shield. The shield of God will protect him from this kind of attack.

We face attacks today. While they may not be as violent as what David faced, they are still violent in their own right. Satan is constantly trying to deliver a knockout blow. It may be mental, physical, emotional, or any number of fronts of attack, but the threat is just as real today as it was in David's time. We are under attack and need God's protection. We need to use His shield and seek refuge in Him.

COMMITMENT

As you face your day, carefully assess the situations you may face. Try to identify where you are weak and where Satan may attack. Then, do as David did, and seek refuge in God. He will protect you, but you must ask Him. You must run to Him. Then He will stand in front of you and block the attacks of Satan.

PRAYER

Lord, today as I look at my day, help me identify where I am weak. Give me the courage to ask for Your help. Help me to hide behind Your shield and trust that You will protect me.

JOURNAL

_____
_____
_____
_____
_____
_____
_____
_____

GRATEFUL

_____
_____
_____
_____
_____
_____
_____
_____

AMENDS

_____
_____
_____
_____
_____
_____
_____
_____

Day 3: Psalm 18:2

• • •

Prayer for Today
God, today grant me
Strength to do as You please,
Wisdom to discern Your best for me,
Compassion to serve others who need You, and
Power to overcome the world's temptations.

BIBLE VERSE

The Lord is my rock and my fortress and my deliverer,
my God, my rock, in whom I take refuge, my shield,
and the horn of my salvation, my stronghold.
—Psalm 18:2 (ESV)

SEEK SHELTER

What a great verse. David, the man after God's own heart, is such a tremendous warrior, and look how he leans on God. Twice in this verse, David refers to God as his rock. He also describes God as his fortress, deliverer, shield, salvation, and stronghold. David's faith and trust in God is complete. It is instructive that David, as a warrior and man after God's own heart, describes the Lord in this way.

When I think of the descriptors for God, I think of a medieval English castle. The castle is made of stone and other strong materials. It is surrounded by a moat and stands there daring unwelcome visitors to enter. It is impossible for enemy soldiers to get in unless the occupant lowers the gate and allows them entry. This also reminds me of the verse in Revelation 3:20 where Jesus says that He is standing at the door and knocking. The only way He can enter our heart is if we make a conscious decision to open the door and let Him in.

APPLICATION

How have you changed? Do you rely on God as Your complete protector like David relied on God? I know I do not. Every day, there are situations that I still try and handle on my own. Sometimes, I think that my concern is too trivial or that God is too busy on more important things. What I fail to recognize in the past, and am now learning, is that God cares for every part of me. He wants to take care of me. The Father wants to be a fortress for me. That paints a very vivid image. His foundation is solid, walls impenetrable, doors that only He can open. It is not a weakness to rely on God. Quite the contrary; it is a strength. David was a tremendous warrior for God, and yet he turned to God for care, protection, and salvation.

COMMITMENT

How is your view of God changing? I look at the life of David and am reminded that it is not a weakness to rely on God. Relying Him is what gets us through the tough times. When we are being pursued from all sides, we still have a safe place where we can run and where we are welcome. Take time today to meditate on what it means to you that God wants to be your rock and your stronghold. Then, make a conscious decision to ask Him to allow you to shelter in the strength of His fortress.

PRAYER

Lord, today help me to be more like David. Help me to run to You as my rock, my fortress, and my stronghold. Remind me daily that life is not meant to be lived alone. Help me learn to trust You and those You put around me for support when I need it.

Journal

_____
_____
_____
_____
_____
_____
_____
_____

Grateful

_____
_____
_____
_____
_____
_____
_____
_____

Amends

_____
_____
_____
_____
_____
_____
_____
_____

Day 4: Psalm 18:30

* * *

Prayer for Today
God, today grant me
Strength to do as You please,
Wisdom to discern Your best for me,
Compassion to serve others who need You, and
Power to overcome the world's temptations.

BIBLE VERSE

> This God—his way is perfect; the word of the Lord proves
> true; he is a shield for all those who take refuge in him.
> —Psalm 18:30 (ESV)

SEEK SHELTER

As I take time to reflect on this chapter of Psalms, I cannot help comparing our experiences with what David faced. My experience is that our society rewards those who help themselves. If things don't go our way, we are encouraged to adjust what we do and keep trying. We are taught, for the most part, to rely on self to ensure safety, prosperity, and health. Yet here is David, a tremendous warrior, putting his complete faith in God. He describes being pursued and God delivering him from his enemies. David's enemies were much stronger and able to pursue him anywhere he went. David tells us how he was not only rescued by God, but the Lord wiped out his enemies. In verse 30, David describes God's way as perfect, and His word is proven to be true. We can count on God's word, and we can count on Him to do what He says He'll do. For that reason, David again refers to God as a shield for those who take refuge in Him.

APPLICATION

God has said He will be our shield. He said it, it is true, and He will do what He says. However, He will not force Himself on us. We must seek Him out. We must walk toward Him and seek the refuge He offers. He loves us and will do anything for us, but it is still our choice. We have no basis for complaint that God is not providing protection if we don't first seek Him out. The other part that is instructive to me is how David refers to God. David honors God's character with his words. He also tells us that he tries to be obedient to God. God will be our refuge if we seek Him. There is no doubt. That is a proven fact. We must seek Him, trust Him, and follow His commands.

COMMITMENT

We all want shelter in tough times. Sometimes, I question why God is not protecting me the way I think He should. When I feel like God is not protecting me, I need to look back at how I am living my life. Am I seeking Him? Am I being obedient to His Word? Am I glorifying and honoring Him as He deserves? I need to make a daily commitment to follow God, be obedient to His words, and then trust that He will provide the protection I need. Our faith is not a works-based faith, but it is a faith based on obedience. We must commit to daily personal obedience to God's Word.

PRAYER

Lord, help me today to be obedient to You. Help me to follow You, live according to Your instructions, and glorify and honor You as You deserve. I trust that You will be a shield of protection for me when I need it.

Journal

_____
_____
_____
_____
_____
_____
_____
_____
_____

Grateful

_____
_____
_____
_____
_____
_____
_____
_____
_____

Amends

_____
_____
_____
_____
_____
_____
_____
_____
_____

Day 5: Psalm 18:35

● ● ●

Prayer for Today
God, today grant me
Strength to do as You please,
Wisdom to discern Your best for me,
Compassion to serve others who need You, and
Power to overcome the world's temptations.

BIBLE VERSE

You have given me the shield of your salvation, and your right
hand supported me, and your gentleness made me great.
—Psalm 18:35 (ESV)

SEEK SHELTER

David reminds us that God gives us three things:

- His shield of salvation
- His right hand of support
- His gentleness

The shield He gives us is His salvation. The shield of a warrior defends against a variety of attacks. In a very real way, that shield also represents the salvation we receive from God. With his shield, a warrior is likely to return from war. Without it, his odds of returning are very low. The shield God provides His children serves the same twofold purpose. We use the shield He provides us to defend against Satan's spiritual attacks. And the shield allows us to withstand attacks and return to Him when our time on this earth is finished. A warrior learns to trust his shield. When will we learn to trust our shield and the One Who provides it to us?

When we are in the thick of the spiritual fight, we need support. When

David faced some of his most difficult battles, he said that the right hand of God supported him. That is a great truth to keep in mind. Spiritual fights are tough. Most times, it seems like a fight of attrition. The first to give up loses. When we feel this tug, we need to dig deep and realize that God is the One Who is supporting us. He alone will carry us through to victory.

And finally, no matter how tough the spiritual fight, we must never lose the gentleness God offers. God's gentleness made David great. How much is His gentleness able to do for you?

APPLICATION

We need to always remember that no matter how difficult the situation is that we face, it is not too great for our God. He is always there to protect us, to lift us up, to support us, and to teach us to be gentle in the face of the most difficult situations. He is a faithful God and a powerful God, but we must seek Him out. He has already provided for us. He has given us everything we need in His Son. We must seek Him out each day.

COMMITMENT

Are you willing to prepare yourself for spiritual battle the way a warrior prepares for physical battle? I have read a number of books about the Navy SEALs. Their training teaches them to be mentally tough. They must have the mental toughness to push through unimaginably difficult situations. We are no different. We must hone our mental and spiritual toughness if we are going to win the spiritual fights that lay ahead. I want to be tough and to win the fight. But, like the Navy SEALS go through intense physical training, we must go through similar spiritual training. We must go through difficult circumstances so that when we take a stand, we are working from muscle memory. Our response to spiritual attack must be hardwired into us.

If we prepare well, our training will kick in, and God will take us through the difficult time we face.

PRAYER

Lord, help me today to begin the spiritual training that will make me spiritually tough. Help me to look at each situation, learn from it, and be strengthened for the next challenge that comes my way.

JOURNAL

_____
_____
_____
_____
_____
_____
_____
_____
_____

GRATEFUL

_____
_____
_____
_____
_____
_____
_____
_____
_____

AMENDS

_____
_____
_____
_____
_____
_____
_____
_____
_____

Day 6: Psalm 28:7

● ● ●

Prayer for Today
God, today grant me
Strength to do as You please,
Wisdom to discern Your best for me,
Compassion to serve others who need You, and
Power to overcome the world's temptations.

BIBLE VERSE

The Lord is my strength and my shield; in him my heart trusts, and I am helped; my heart exults, and with my song I give thanks to him.
—Psalm 28:7 (ESV)

SEEK SHELTER

Again, in this verse, we see David declaring that God is his strength and his shield. David knew that no matter where he was or what situation he found himself in, God would provide for his safety. More than that, David trusted God in his heart. To his very core, David knew that he could trust the Lord and that He would help him. Further, God's strength and shield caused David to lift Him up, to sing to Him, and to give thanks to Him. When we have faith like David, we have the confidence that God will protect us.

David's faith grew to where it was not just head knowledge; it was heart knowledge. It is easy to know, in your mind, that something is true. It is a completely different matter when you know in your heart that it's true. Heart knowledge has a tremendous impact on the life of a believer. When we get to a point where we know that God and His promises are true, in our heart, then and only then will His words begin to have an impact on who we are and how we live. Heart knowledge changes the fabric of who we are.

APPLICATION

So how do we achieve heart knowledge? It sounds simple enough, but it can be a struggle. We must come to terms with the fact that we need a Savior. We must know and understand that we need God. But more than that, and perhaps most importantly, we need to learn how to trust God. One word: trust. We must get to a point where, like David, we can say "in him my heart trusts." Trust is a learned behavior. Intellectually, we may know something is true, but until we learn to trust that truth, we may continue to live dangerously and perhaps even recklessly. By way of example, you could say that you believe in the law of gravity. But if you do not trust that law in your heart, you might still decide to walk off a high surface and suddenly find yourself rocketing toward the ground. It is too late to trust at that point.

COMMITMENT

Are you ready to begin to take a leap of faith? Today, you need to begin to read God's words and really seek out their meaning. How can you apply His truth to the way you live? If you begin to view God's Word in this manner, then you will learn to trust Him. You will learn to trust Him when you begin to see fundamental changes in how you live your life. Your trust in Him will continue to grow as You see His promises being fulfilled in your life. Then you will know that your heart and your life are changing. When you can live life trusting God, you will experience freedom like never before.

PRAYER

Lord, help me to begin trusting You in my heart today. Help my trust in You to grow. Help me begin to see the change in the fabric of who You are molding me to be.

JOURNAL

_____
_____
_____
_____
_____
_____
_____
_____
_____

GRATEFUL

_____
_____
_____
_____
_____
_____
_____
_____
_____

AMENDS

_____
_____
_____
_____
_____
_____
_____
_____
_____

Day 7: Psalm 33:20

• • •

Prayer for Today
God, today grant me
Strength to do as You please,
Wisdom to discern Your best for me,
Compassion to serve others who need You, and
Power to overcome the world's temptations.

BIBLE VERSE

Our soul waits for the Lord; he is our help and our shield.
—Psalm 33:20 (ESV)

SEEK SHELTER

I really like this verse. I like the simplicity and the depth. The waiting the psalmist describes is soul-deep. Waiting is not something we do well. Since the beginning of time, people have been impatient. We tend to take the approach that if God will not do what we want, then we'll take matters into our own hands. How many times has that worked out? If we are completely honest, not many. In a moment of brutal honesty, when we look at what we think we have done well, the results have been marginal at best, at least compared to what God could have done on our behalf. The sad part to me is that we will never really know what God could have done because we got impatient and pushed our own agenda forward, ignoring Him.

The reward for learning to wait is made crystal-clear in this verse. When we learn to wait, God is our help and our shield. That sounds easy. Reflect on that hard, though. He is our help and our shield. There is absolutely nothing that can get in the way of God's will. And sometimes His will is that we struggle so we learn to trust Him and rely on Him more.

APPLICATION

We must train our soul to wait. We are not born with the ability; it is learned. Learning to wait requires us to learn how to be patient, another character trait we are not born with. That said, when we learn how to be patient and to wait, the results are beyond what we can imagine. I am not as patient as I need to be, and I am not always great at waiting. But I am learning. God is teaching me to be patient and wait. The results have been beyond my wildest expectations. I am helping to start a company, and we've had financial challenges; people have asked me if I should give up on it. Every time we run out of money or an approval is delayed, the questions start almost immediately. Through this situation, I have tried hard to be patient and wait. I have been down to my last dollar more than once, but every time, God has answered.

COMMITMENT

Are you ready to commit to the ability to wait? It will definitely test your patience. When you make this commitment, you will be tested and tried in ways you cannot imagine. Not that you will be perfect, but if you allow yourself to be trained by the situations God places in front of you, you will also be blessed in ways you cannot imagine. Our God is a big God Who thinks much bigger thoughts than we can comprehend.

PRAYER

Lord, help me today to commit to learning how to wait on You. Help me to diligently seek You, wait on You, and see how You will work.

Journal

_____
_____
_____
_____
_____
_____
_____
_____

Grateful

_____
_____
_____
_____
_____
_____
_____
_____

Amends

_____
_____
_____
_____
_____
_____
_____
_____

STEP 6 • • • • • • • •

Run the Race

Therefore, if anyone is in Christ, he is a new creation. The
old has passed away; behold, the new has come.
—2 Corinthians 5:17 (ESV)

Achieving Long-Term Sobriety •••

Long-term sobriety can be achieved, but it takes a lot of work. Satan will
use any means at his disposal to interrupt your sobriety and send you back
to your drug of choice. You must always be aware and stay on the lookout
for the triggers Satan uses to drive you back to your old ways. Our best
and only defense is to know God's Word. The verse mentioned above has
become one of my favorites in sobriety. For me, the biggest attack I face
is Satan reminding me of my past. He uses my past to try to convince me
that God could never use a guy like me to further His kingdom. But look
at what Paul tells the Corinthians. When we become Christians, we are a
new creation. Our old self has passed away and we become new in His eyes.

This is a fantastic verse to commit to memory and use for those times
when Satan attempts to use your past life to derail your new life.

One of the measuring sticks I use to gauge my faith and how close I
am walking with God is to assess how often Satan attacks me. It never
fails; the closer I try to walk with God, the more intense the attacks
from the evil one. He prowls about looking for someone he can devour.
Nothing pleases him more than attacking a person who is trying to walk
with God.

Living Life

● ● ●

In one of my first AA meetings after I graduated from therapy, one of the old-timers told me, "You don't have to relapse; you can be one and done." Long-term sobriety depends on your commitment to the program and willingness to work for the freedom that comes from sobriety. Sobriety is more than not drinking, not using, and not getting high or drunk. It is about making a commitment to live a spiritual life outlined for us in the Bible. God gives us the pathway; we just have to follow it.

In terms of living life going forward, Jesus gives us the best advice of all. In John 8:11, Jesus tells the woman to "go … sin no more." We will be successfully free of addiction when we learn to go and sin no more. It is hard for me to think of alcohol and addiction as sin. But at the end of the day, that is exactly what it is. Taking the first drink is a decision that I make. Once I take the first drink, then the addiction kicks in, and I cannot stop at just one drink. In a sense, the disease kicks in after I make a bad decision to take the first drink.

The hardest part of living this new life is learning how to deal with stress. We are all asked to take note of the triggers that sent us to the cabinet to pour the first drink. These triggers are the exact things that Satan will use to try and tempt you back into your old ways. Especially in the early days, you must always be on guard and aware of your surroundings. One of the keys to long-term success is to create your exit plan for each situation before you find yourself in that situation.

Developing your tactical plan now and practicing how you will engage that plan is critical. The more you practice engaging that plan, the easier it is to follow it when you really need it. Just look at elite athletes as an example. They practice diligently over extended periods of time. When they get in a game, they don't have to think about the fundamentals. Muscle memory kicks in, and they play at their peak. The spiritual life is no different. We need to practice spiritual fundamentals now so they become spiritual muscle memory when we need it.

Seek Purpose

● ● ●

After I got sober, I came to realize that my life, toward the end of my drinking career, lacked purpose. In 2006, I was nominated to *Indianapolis*

Business Journal's Indianapolis Forty Under 40 list. They closed my interview in that paper with a quote that I provided to the interviewer when asked about advice I would provide to a person wanting to achieve success in business. At the time, my answer was "It's not about chasing dollar bills. It's about doing what you enjoy." Eight short years later, I realized that I was not taking my own advice. I was on a treadmill, running as fast as I could to see how much I could make. My life lacked genuine purpose.

The lack of purpose was caused by my lack of faith. I had wandered from the faith that had guided me for so many years. In Luke 15, we read the account of the prodigal son. He took his inheritance and went off to spend it on high living, wasting both time and resources. The prodigal son left his family to experience the best of what the world had to offer. What he learned, after his resources ran out, is that you cannot buy happiness.

When we try to find pleasure in the things the world has to offer, it is fun for a season. But in every case, that road ends. It may end while you are still on this earth, but it will definitely end when you die. What we all find at the end of the earthly road to pleasure is a dead end. Eventually, we come to the end of that road, and there is nothing left to find. In the end, all the world has to offer us is empty, hollow promises. I know. I found the end of that road.

In 2014, I hit the end of my road to pleasure. It was the darkest, loneliest time of my life. I had almost no friends, lost most of my money, and nearly lost my family. I was completely and utterly without hope or purpose. Fortunately, God is a loving and forgiving Father when we stray from His path and His family. Like the prodigal son, I was getting what I needed to get by in the pig trough of life. But you know what? When I came to the end of that road and realized it was empty, God welcomed me back. He was standing there, waiting to welcome me back into His family and provide my life with the purpose that He intended.

Meditate on the Word   ● ● ●

I will meditate on your precepts and fix my eyes on your ways.
—Psalm 119:15 (ESV)

This Book of the Law shall not depart from your mouth, but you
shall meditate on it day and night, so that you may be careful to
do according to all that is written in it. For then you will make
your way prosperous, and then you will have good success.
—Joshua 1:8 (ESV)

Practice these things, immerse yourself in them,
so that all may see your progress.
—1 Timothy 4:15 (ESV)

I love these verses. So much can be solved when I start by fixing my mind
in the right areas. The mind is where backsliding begins. It is where Satan
attacks. Think about it. Satan plants seeds of doubt in your mind. He causes
you to question your faith. He causes you to question your worth to God.
He causes you to question whether God can even use a person like you.
This can all be overcome by keeping your eyes on Him and on His ways.

Dictionary.com defines the word *meditation* as "to engage in thought or
contemplation; reflect." Throughout the Psalms, the psalmist uses the word
meditate. We need to be constantly thinking about and reflecting on God.

In the Old Testament, Joshua was instructed to always speak according
to the Book of the Law. He was instructed to meditate on the Book of the
Law, day and night. Why? God wanted Joshua's mind to be completely
focused on Him. He wanted Joshua to speak continually of Him, and
Joshua could only do that if he immersed himself in God's words. By
completely immersing himself in God's words, he would make himself
prosperous. Prosperity can mean many things. It's not just financial or
material; most importantly, it is spiritual.

We see a similar admonition in the New Testament. Paul writes to Timothy
and instructs him to practice these things and to be immersed in them Paul is
speaking about the public reading of scripture, exhortation, and teaching. We
must care for our own faith by spending time with God. We need to apply His
life principles to the life He's given us. Then we need to share what the Lord
is doing in us and for us with others. The Christian life is complete, and the
race is run well, when we share what God is doing for us with others. When
we do that, we fulfill the great commission at the end of Matthew 28:18–20,
where Jesus tells us to go and make disciples of all nations.

Accept the Rest Jesus Offers ● ● ●

> Come to me, all who labor and are heavy laden, and I will
> give you rest. Take my yoke upon you, and learn from me,
> for I am gentle and lowly in heart, and you will find rest for
> your souls. For my yoke is easy, and my burden is light.
> —Matthew 11:28–30 (ESV)

Why do you think Jesus offers us rest? Why do you think He tells us that His yoke is easy and His burden is light? Because Jesus lived among us for thirty-three years, and He knows just how difficult and cruel life can be. Remember when He went into the wilderness to be tempted by Satan (Matthew 4)? Jesus was all alone with Satan and fasted for forty days and forty nights. He was exhausted and very hungry. He had not eaten in nearly seven weeks. At the end of this time of testing, Satan really ramped up his attack. I can imagine the tone of voice Satan uses, sneering and talking down to Jesus.

But take careful note of how Jesus responded in the temptations that are shared with us. Satan was twisting God's words and taking them out of context. Satan was using God's words to say things He never intended. But Jesus knew His Father so well that He was able to rebuke Satan with the true words of God.

Satan will attack us in the same way. He will wait until we are at our weakest, and then he will use God's own words to speak lies and falsehoods. Satan is a master manipulator, and we must always be prepared with God's words. God's Word is the only offensive weapon we have to beat back the lies of Satan.

Pray Unceasingly ● ● ●

> Do not be anxious about anything, but in everything by prayer and
> supplication with thanksgiving let your requests be made known
> to God. And the peace of God, which surpasses all understanding,
> will guard your hearts and your minds in Christ Jesus.
> —Philippians 4:6–7 (ESV)

If I have learned anything on this journey, it is the value of prayer. Jesus prayed publicly, and He prayed privately. He prayed at times that were inconvenient to Him personally (early in the morning or late at night). He prayed short prayers, and He prayed long prayers. But I learned that He prayed continually, just as Paul was instructing the Philippians. Jesus knew God the Father, in part because He is the Son, but also because He developed a relationship with the Father. God speaks to us through His Word; we speak to Him through our times of prayer. It is fine to ask God for the things we think we need, but we must also ask Him to provide what He knows we need. There is a huge difference.

Now look at how Paul instructs the Philippians regarding prayer. He tells them not to be anxious about anything. Anxiety filled almost every aspect of my life during my addiction. That is one way that Satan separates us from God. Paul also tells them to pray in every situation and to be thankful. I have heard Rick Warren say, and it is true, that God asks us to pray about everything and be thankful. We do not have to be thankful *about* everything, but we do have to be thankful *in* everything. God calls us to be thankful even when times are tough because in those tough times, He stretches us. Those tough times, in the end, draw us closer to Him and make us stronger witnesses for Him. Am I thankful for my addiction? Not really. But am I thankful in my recovery from addiction? Absolutely. Because I have walked through the pain of addiction, I can relate to others in a similar situation. It is a gift of God to be used to reach others.

Remember You Are a New Creation ● ● ●

> Therefore, if anyone is in Christ, he is a new creation. The
> old has passed away; behold, the new has come.
> —2 Corinthians 5:17 (ESV)

At all times, you must remember you are a new creation. Look at how Paul describes our new life to the Corinthians. The old self has passed away, and now we are new. What happens when our bodies pass away on this earth? We bury them. We bury the dead bodies, and we never see that body again while we are on this earth. Dead people who are believers will have a new heavenly body. Once people have their new heavenly body, they won't look at their old body and say, "See who I was." No. That old body has passed away, and we are focused on the new. So it is with our faith. When we decide to leave the old life behind, it is dead and buried. It is out of mind. We should be focused on the new creation that God has made us and the work He wants to do through our new life.

Go Forth and Run with Purpose   ● ● ●

Now it is time to put all this learning into action. God has taken this time to remind us of everything He has done for us. He has done more on our behalf than we'll ever know. What we do know is that He has given us the chance to run,, with purpose, the race that lies ahead. We must be constantly focused on the finish line. We must constantly train. We must remain focused on God. If we can remain focused on Him, He can work wonders through each one of us.

Weekly Plan   ● ● ●

- Day 1: 1 Corinthians 9:24–25a
- Day 2: Philippians 2:14–16
- Day 3: Hebrews 12:1–2
- Day 4: 1 Peter 4:4
- Day 5: Psalm 119:32
- Day 6: Matthew 11:28–30
- Day 7: 2 Corinthians 5:17

Day 1: 1 Corinthians 9:24–25a

* * *

Prayer for Today
God, today grant me
Strength to do as You please,
Wisdom to discern Your best for me,
Compassion to serve others who need You, and
Power to overcome the world's temptations.

BIBLE VERSE

Do you not know that in a race all the runners run, but
only one receives the prize? So run that you may obtain
it. Every athlete exercises self-control in all things.
—1 Corinthians 9:24–25a (ESV)

RUN THE RACE

To run the race of the Christian life, we must run with purpose and
exercise self-control. I know several people who are runners. They didn't
wake up one morning and decide to go run a marathon. They spend time
training. Training for a race is hard work. They must maintain their focus
over a long period of time. Prior to the race, their daily focus is on getting
to the starting line. Everything they do as they train is focused on making
them the best runner they can be.

They also display tremendous self-control. It is easy to decide to sleep
in, watch a television show, or have an extra dessert. But those who want
to be competitive give these things up in order to stick to their training
program. They demonstrate self-control in every aspect of life.

APPLICATION

Why train so hard? Because as they train, they build up their muscles. They also develop the focus that is required to finish a race strong. They begin their training slowly at first, and then they add distance. As they add distance, they begin to focus on time. Gradually, with practice, runners develop from soft average people into people who are both physically and mentally fit. After months of training, they are prepared to run their race. After they get to the starting line, their focus shifts. Now the focus is on the finish line. All the discipline that has been developed over the previous months is now poured into the race ahead of them.

The Christian life is no different. The Christian life is not a sprint; it is a marathon. Sure, there are times when we must sprint, but overall, the Christian life is a long-distance run. The only way to be successful in the Christian life is to maintain a focus on the finish line. For us as Christians, the goal line is at the end of our days, looking back at a life well lived. More importantly, is a life well lived for Christ and crossing the finish line into eternity with God, His Son, and the Holy Spirit.

COMMITMENT

Are you ready to begin training for the marathon of life? If so, spend time with God in His Word every day. As you read, focus on what the words mean to you and the life that is being built in you. Set attainable goals, but allow God to help you stretch your goals. Prepare to stretch and strain. He will mold you into the person He wants you to be, but it takes time and the pain of training to achieve His best for your life.

PRAYER

Lord, today I want to begin training for the race of life. Build within me the discipline that is required as I begin to train for the life You want for me. Help me to endure the challenges that are placed before me so I can run the race of life with purpose.

JOURNAL

_____
_____
_____
_____
_____
_____
_____
_____
_____

GRATEFUL

_____
_____
_____
_____
_____
_____
_____
_____
_____

AMENDS

_____
_____
_____
_____
_____
_____
_____
_____
_____

Day 2: Philippians 2:14–16

● ● ●

Prayer for Today
God, today grant me
Strength to do as You please,
Wisdom to discern Your best for me,
Compassion to serve others who need You, and
Power to overcome the world's temptations.

BIBLE VERSE

Do all things without grumbling or disputing, that you may be blameless and innocent, children of God without blemish in the midst of a crooked and twisted generation, among whom you shine as lights in the world, holding fast to the word of life, so that in the day of Christ I may be proud that I did not run in vain or labor in vain.
—Philippians 2:14–16 (ESV)

RUN THE RACE

This section of Philippians starts with a statement telling us that we are to do all things without grumbling or disputing. It doesn't say some things or only the things you agree with. It says in all things. Now obviously, that doesn't mean that we are to do things that are illegal, unethical, immoral, and the like. But for the things that are otherwise right, we are to do them and not argue. This is tough. It seems that we are all born with the argument gene on prominent display. How many times have we told our kids not to argue, "just do what I say"? It would be the first phrase taught in parent school, if there were such a thing. God tells us not to be argumentative because He knows that is what is best for us.

So the question becomes why we should be agreeable and not argumentative. Because God wants each of us to be blameless, innocent, and without blemish. That is a high calling. He wants the absolute best for each of us. Notice how Paul describes the world. He calls the world crooked and twisted. Those two traits of the world remain true today. But when we are agreeable and not argumentative, look at what happens. We shine as lights in the world. Our world today needs good lights and examples of clean living. I cannot think of a greater goal or higher calling in our world today.

Our world today needs good lights and examples of clean living.

APPLICATION

We need to make an effort to do things without complaining. And some days it takes a lot of effort. But when we are agreeable it is not just the world that benefits. Being agreeable benefits us as well. Look at what Paul says we will receive by being agreeable. By learning to be agreeable, I can then be proud when I meet Christ that I did not run or labor in vain. The opposite of that is true as well. By being argumentative we risk doing the things we do in vain. People will not listen when we argue about everything. In fact, they may be turned away from us, and worse, possibly turn away from saving faith in Jesus. People are won by a softer spirit.

COMMITMENT

As we think about running the good race, we need to make a commitment to do as Paul instructs in verse 14. We must do all things without grumbling or disputing. It is tough, but as you become more agreeable, be aware of the impact it has on the people around you.

PRAYER

Lord, sometimes being agreeable is not easy, but it is what You ask us to do. Help me to learn to be more agreeable in my walk with You.

Journal

_____
_____
_____
_____
_____
_____
_____
_____
_____

Grateful

_____
_____
_____
_____
_____
_____
_____
_____
_____

Amends

_____
_____
_____
_____
_____
_____
_____
_____
_____

Day 3: Hebrews 12:1–2

● ● ●

Prayer for Today
God, today grant me
Strength to do as You please,
Wisdom to discern Your best for me,
Compassion to serve others who need You, and
Power to overcome the world's temptations.

BIBLE VERSE

Therefore, since we are surrounded by so great a cloud of witnesses,
let us also lay aside every weight, and sin which clings so closely,
and let us run with endurance the race that is set before us,
looking to Jesus, the founder and perfecter of our faith, who for
the joy that was set before him endured the cross, despising the
shame, and is seated at the right hand of the throne of God.
—Hebrews 12:1–2 (ESV)

RUN THE RACE

This verse gives us a great picture of what it looks like to run the race of
life. We have Jesus to show us how we should run. He alone ran the perfect
race and is now seated at the right hand of God's throne. Jesus continually
looked to His Father for direction in His daily life. No matter what He was
asked to do, He did it without question. In these verses, He tells us how
we can run a satisfying life race. Like Jesus, we need to be focused on His
Father. We need to do as we are asked without questioning. So how do we
hear His voice? Through time spent with Him in His Word. He speaks to
us through His Word, the Bible. Everything we need to live a successful
life is contained in His words. We just need to take time with Him to read,
meditate, and spend time listening to His words.

Application

Think about every sprint or long-distance race you've seen. Were any runners carrying additional weight? Not likely. In fact, runners train in a way that makes them physically fit and at the lightest possible weight. They carry no extra baggage with them. They bring the essentials to the race. In the same way, Jesus tells us that we need to lay aside every weight and sin that is trying to stick to us. Satan uses the weight of our sin to slow us down and hopes to take us out of the race all together. We cannot give this victory to Satan.

If we run with purpose, focused on Jesus, we will run a successful life race. The key is to always be looking at the race that is before us, not behind us. This is so critical. We cannot run an effective race if we are constantly looking over our shoulder. When we do that, we allow Satan to distract us with thoughts of weaknesses and sins that are in the past and completely forgiven by God. God wants us to always be focused on the race ahead. There is not one part of the past we can change, so why think about it?

The key is to always be looking at the race that is before us, not behind us.

Commitment

Dear friends, make a commitment today to put your past behind you and leave it there. God is not concerned about the past. If we confess and ask forgiveness, He forgives us completely. He only cares about our future and what we do with the rest of our lives. Make a commitment today to live each day looking forward to the race ahead. Train so that you can run with endurance, because life throws a lot at us.

Prayer

Lord, thank You for Your words today. Help me not to look at my past, but rather focus fully and completely on the race You have laid before me. Help me to run with endurance the race You have designed for me.

Day 4: 1 Peter 4:4

* * *

Prayer for Today
God, today grant me
Strength to do as You please,
Wisdom to discern Your best for me,
Compassion to serve others who need You, and
Power to overcome the world's temptations.

BIBLE VERSE

With respect to this they are surprised when you do not join
them in the same flood of debauchery, and they malign you.
—1 Peter 4:4 (ESV)

RUN THE RACE

It is not good enough to just run the race of life. We must run it with
integrity. Runners who are found to have broken the rules are disqualified
from the race. They must be honest and run according to the rules.
Likewise, God asks us to follow Him when we run the race of life. When
we look at verse 4 in the context of verses 1–6, we find that Peter is telling
people that the time for their sins has since passed. In 1 Peter 4:3, Peter
lists a number of sins that plague most of us before our conversion to Jesus.
The list he presents is a long one, but it is not exhaustive.

We all have things in the past that we wish were not there. There is
nothing we can do about the past. Look at how Peter begins verse 3: "The
time is past." He knows that we all have things hidden in our past. He is
telling us that is okay, as long as we leave them there. At the point of our
conversion, we decide to leave that lifestyle behind. People will notice a
change in us after we experience a conversion to Christian living.

APPLICATION

It is critical to understand that people will see us differently, not because of what we say as much as what we do and how we act. When we have a conversion experience, people may watch us closely to see if we act differently. They are searching us to see if our conversion is genuine and real or if it is all for show. How we act speaks far more loudly about who we have become than any words can ever express. In 1 Peter 4:6, Peter tells us why it is so important to live a new life, not just talk a new life. The Gospel was preached so that people would see the soul-deep change in us and want what we have. He wants us to live apart from our past so that others may live in the spirit, the way God does.

COMMITMENT

Friends, have you experienced a true conversion to Jesus? Does your life look different today? Make a commitment today that your life will begin to reflect the new values that inhabit you because of your faith in Him. Don't just talk about who you've become. Let people see who you've become. We all have things in our past we're not proud of. But those are often the very things that allow us to reach others for Him.

Don't just talk about who you've become. Let people see who you've become.

PRAYER

Lord, help me today to live my life the way You want me to live it. Help my actions to speak louder than my words. Let those around me see that I am different. Use me to reach others for Your kingdom today.

Journal

_____
_____
_____
_____
_____
_____
_____
_____

Grateful

_____
_____
_____
_____
_____
_____
_____
_____

Amends

_____
_____
_____
_____
_____
_____
_____
_____
_____

Day 5: Psalm 119:32

• • •

Prayer for Today
God, today grant me
Strength to do as You please,
Wisdom to discern Your best for me,
Compassion to serve others who need You, and
Power to overcome the world's temptations.

BIBLE VERSE

I will run in the way of your commandments
when you enlarge my heart!
—Psalm 119:32 (ESV)

RUN THE RACE

To understand this verse, you must read the verses that come before it. Look at Psalm 119:25–32, and take to heart the prayer of the psalmist. He is looking to God for understanding, strength, learning, and faithfulness. He wants to get closer to God. In verse 27, the psalmist says that he will meditate on God's wondrous works. And in verse 31, he says that he will cling to God's testimonies. Why does he say these things? Because he does not want to be put to shame. The psalmist wants to follow God and His commands. He wants to learn all that God has to teach him so he can live a life pleasing to Him.

APPLICATION

It sounds so easy to say that we want to follow God and His commands. But we need to step back and take a deeply honest assessment of our lives and our commitment to Him. In my own life, I had to realize that alcohol had become the most important thing to me. I spent every waking moment planning my next drink. I made sure that there was enough alcohol around so I wouldn't get caught short when the stores were closed. I think where I would be today if I had put a fraction of that effort toward seeking God.

These verses are not intended to place a burden on us. Rather, it is a joy to get to know God. I look at my life and realize that there are plenty of opportunities to spend more time with God. I must decide between God and other pursuits. It is fine to have hobbies and outlets, but not if they take me away from my relationship with Him. If we are going to run the race of life successfully, we must always keep God and His teachings in the front of our mind. We cannot afford to engage in activities that get in the way of our relationship with Him.

The successful race is run when we run the race the way He wants us to run.

COMMITMENT

Make a commitment today to spend more time with God. He wants to have a relationship with you. Relationships are a two-way street. God wants to spend time with us, but we need to be willing to spend time with Him. We do that by reading His Word, reflecting on His Word, and meditating on His Word. Only then will we know how He wants us to run the race.

PRAYER

Lord, give me the strength to focus on You today. Help me to spend time with You in the reading of Your Word, meditation on its meaning, and focus on the application of Your truth in my life. Lord, I want to serve You in a way that is pleasing to You. I want to run the race focused forward on You and Your desire for my life.

JOURNAL

_____
_____
_____
_____
_____
_____
_____
_____
_____

GRATEFUL

_____
_____
_____
_____
_____
_____
_____
_____
_____

AMENDS

_____
_____
_____
_____
_____
_____
_____
_____
_____

Day 6: Matthew 11:28–30

• • •

Prayer for Today
God, today grant me
Strength to do as You please,
Wisdom to discern Your best for me,
Compassion to serve others who need You, and
Power to overcome the world's temptations.

BIBLE VERSE

Come to me, all who labor and are heavy laden, and I will
give you rest. Take my yoke upon you, and learn from me,
for I am gentle and lowly in heart, and you will find rest for
your souls. For my yoke is easy, and my burden is light.
—Matthew 11:28–30 (ESV)

RUN THE RACE

How many of us, toward the end of our addiction career, were completely
exhausted? I know I was. To drink the way I drank and maintain a job
and family was completely exhausting. For many of us, our burdens ran
deep long before we took that first drink or used the first drug. Addiction
for many of us is a way to escape burdens that we can no longer bear. If
the burden will not go away, then at least that drink or drug will help me
forget even if only for a little bit. At the end of a long day, the drink that
I took allowed me to get to sleep and face another day. Gradually, as my
body grew accustomed to the alcohol, it took more to achieve the same
effect. The slide was so gradual. Eventually, I looked back and realized that
the alcohol had become a crutch, and it could no longer perform for me
the way it did in the early days.

APPLICATION

The problem that many of us face is that we internalize many of our fears and burdens. As a result, we often suffer from anxiety and depression. Alcohol and drugs become a way to self-medicate. Eventually, though, these fears catch up with us. I look at these verses and realize just how much Jesus cares about me and how much He wants to help. At every turn in the Bible, I see Jesus standing there with His arms outstretched, waiting for me. But, you see, the real problem is that I must take the first step toward Him. He can only do so much. Recovery from addiction will never happen unless we want it for ourselves. We are the only ones who can take the step and say, "I have a problem."

The Christian life is the same way. We must humble ourselves, take that first step toward Jesus, and admit that we have a problem. Look at who Jesus is addressing in verse 28: all who labor and are heavy laden. Does that describe you? But look at how He bookends that description: "Come to me … and I will give you rest." I can tell you from personal experience, after more than a few days of sobriety, the rest He offers is far greater than any other rest you can experience in this life. Will you take that first step toward Jesus? He is waiting for you and wants to give you rest. And the rest He offers is not just physical rest. He offers us the opportunity to find rest for our souls. There is no better rest.

COMMITMENT

Will you make a commitment, do as Jesus asks, and come to Him? You are the only one who can make that decision and take that step. The first step is a huge one. It is tough because you must humble yourself and admit that you cannot continue on your own. But once you make that decision and take that step, you will never want to turn back.

PRAYER

Lord, help me today to make a commitment to do as You ask and come to You. It is difficult for me because I must humble myself and admit that I cannot handle life on my own. I recognize that I need You and that I need the rest that only You can offer.

Journal

_____
_____
_____
_____
_____
_____
_____
_____
_____

Grateful

_____
_____
_____
_____
_____
_____
_____
_____
_____

Amends

_____
_____
_____
_____
_____
_____
_____
_____
_____

Day 7: 2 Corinthians 5:17

● ● ●

Prayer for Today
God, today grant me
Strength to do as You please,
Wisdom to discern Your best for me,
Compassion to serve others who need You, and
Power to overcome the world's temptations.

BIBLE VERSE

Therefore, if anyone is in Christ, he is a new creation. The
old has passed away; behold, the new has come.
—2 Corinthians 5:17 (ESV)

RUN THE RACE

When we finally decide to run the race that God has place before us, we will experience a freedom like we've never experienced before. This last verse in the Pathway to Recovery toolbox may be the most important verse of all the verses we studied. Why do I say this? Because the minute you decide to follow God, Satan kicks his attacks into high gear. He will come at you with everything he has. I can tell you from personal experience that one of his favorite attacks is to dismiss your personal worth to God. Satan will flood your mind with thoughts that take you back to who you were. He will use those thoughts to then drill into your mind that God cannot use someone as broken as you, someone who has made the mistakes you've made. Don't let Satan have that opening into your life.

As we look at the people in the Bible, we must realize they all had flaws. David committed adultery. Paul persecuted the church. Peter denied Jesus three times. The list is long. But look at how God has used these people throughout history. He makes His church strong through our weaknesses. Our weaknesses are what allow us to reach others with the hope that can only be found in Him. If I were not an alcoholic, I would not be able to identify with and help other addicts. Every single time Satan tries to attack me because of my past, I need to remember this verse. The old me has passed away. That part of my life is dead. The new me now has an opportunity to serve Him and support His plan.

APPLICATION

Satan does not want me to believe that God is willing to provide for my salvation. He wants me to constantly be reminded of how I failed God in the past and how that past failure will guarantee future failure. This verse speaks the opposite to me. When I repent of my sins, I am forgiven. I am a new creation. The old has passed away. My life of sinfulness is behind me. It is dead and buried permanently. God gives me a chance to be completely new in Him.

COMMITMENT

Will you commit this verse to memory? You will need it when Satan decides to attack your character and your past. Satan will come at you with everything he can. Look at Job. Satan destroyed him completely. But over time, Job recognized the goodness of God, and God blessed him. He will do the same for you.

PRAYER

Lord, help me to remember today that I am a new creation. My past has been laid to rest, and I am free of that bondage. Thank You for making me a new creation. Help me to serve You in all I do.

Journal

_____
_____
_____
_____
_____
_____
_____
_____
_____

Grateful

_____
_____
_____
_____
_____
_____
_____
_____
_____

Amends

_____
_____
_____
_____
_____
_____
_____
_____
_____

Concluding Thoughts

If you are reading this, then you have covered a lot of ground in the last six weeks. I hope you feel a bit more secure in both your sobriety and your Christian walk. The last six weeks was not easy. I know because I've been there. The first forty days or so were the absolute worst for me. When you decide to take your addiction head-on, it is a tremendous battle. Many days, I felt like I just wouldn't make it. I wanted to give up. But I had people around me who helped me succeed. So much of your daily life must change. Those changes are hard, but they are worth the fight. The rewards are eternal.

I keep going back to the words of the old-timer at one of my first AA meetings. He said, "You don't have to relapse; you can be one and done." Well, you can be one and done also. You just have to be willing to fight the good fight. The only way you can fight the good fight is to trust God, lean on Him, and accept what He has to offer. You will not be disappointed.

Faith-Based Recovery Toolbox

RECONCILIATION

All this is from God, who through Christ reconciled us to himself and gave us the ministry of reconciliation; that is, in Christ God was reconciling the world to himself, not counting their trespasses against them, and entrusting to us the message of reconciliation. Therefore, we are ambassadors for Christ, God making his appeal through us. We implore you on behalf of Christ, be reconciled to God.
—2 CORINTHIANS 5:18–20 (ESV)

For if while we were enemies we were reconciled to God by the death of his Son, much more, now that we are reconciled, shall we be saved by his life.
—ROMANS 5:10 (ESV)

And might reconcile us both to God in one body through the cross, thereby killing the hostility.
—EPHESIANS 2:16 (ESV)

And not only this, but we also exult in God through our Lord Jesus Christ, through whom we have now received the reconciliation.
—ROMANS 5:11 (NASB)

For in him all the fullness of God was pleased to dwell, 20 and through him to reconcile to himself all things, whether on earth or in heaven, making peace by the blood of his cross.
—COLOSSIANS 1:19–20 (ESV)

For if their rejection is the reconciliation of the world, what will their acceptance be but life from the dead?

—Romans 11:15 (NASB)

You, however, are not in the flesh but in the Spirit, if in fact the Spirit of God dwells in you. Anyone who does not have the Spirit of Christ does not belong to him.

—Romans 8:9 (ESV)

Repentance

Repent, therefore, of this wickedness of yours, and pray to the Lord that, if possible, the intent of your heart may be forgiven you.

—Acts 8:22 (ESV)

From that time Jesus began to preach, saying, "Repent, for the kingdom of heaven is at hand."

—Matthew 4:17 (ESV)

No, I tell you; but unless you repent, you will all likewise perish.

—Luke 13:3 (ESV)

And Peter said to them, "Repent and be baptized every one of you in the name of Jesus Christ for the forgiveness of your sins, and you will receive the gift of the Holy Spirit.

—Acts 2:38 (ESV)

Now after John was arrested, Jesus came into Galilee, proclaiming the gospel of God, 15 and saying, "The time is fulfilled, and the kingdom of God is at hand; repent and believe in the gospel."

—Mark 1:14–15 (ESV)

Or do you presume on the riches of His kindness and forbearance and patience, not knowing that God's kindness is meant to lead you to repentance?

—Romans 2:4 (ESV)

For godly grief produces repentance that leads to salvation without regret, whereas worldly grief produces death.

—2 Corinthians 7:10 (ESV)

Faith

He said to them, "Because of your little faith. For truly, I say to you, if you have faith like a grain of mustard seed, you will say to this mountain, 'Move from here to there,' and it will move, and nothing will be impossible for you." And he said to the woman, "Your faith has saved you; go in peace."

—Luke 7:50 (ESV)

And what they said pleased the whole gathering, and they chose Stephen, a man full of faith and of the Holy Spirit, and Philip, and Prochorus, and Nicanor, and Timon, and Parmenas, and Nicolaus, a proselyte of Antioch.

—Acts 6:5 (ESV)

Therefore, since we have been justified by faith, we have peace with God through our Lord Jesus Christ.

—Romans 5:1 (ESV)

So we are always of good courage. We know that while we are at home in the body we are away from the Lord, for we walk by faith, not by sight.

—2 Corinthians 5:6–7 (ESV)

For by grace you have been saved through faith. And this is not your own doing; it is the gift of God.

—Ephesians 2:8 (ESV)

But let him ask in faith, with no doubting, for the one who doubts is like a wave of the sea that is driven and tossed by the wind.

—James 1:6 (ESV)

God's Armor

Therefore take up the whole armor of God, that you may be able to withstand in the evil day, and having done all, to stand firm.
—Ephesians 6:13 (ESV)

Stand therefore, having fastened on the belt of truth.
—Ephesians 6:14a (ESV)

And having put on the breastplate of righteousness.
—Ephesians 6:14b (ESV)

And, as shoes for your feet, having put on the readiness given by the gospel of peace.
—Ephesians 6:15 (ESV)

In all circumstances take up the shield of faith, with which you can extinguish all the flaming darts of the evil one.
Ephesians 6:16 (ESV)

And take the helmet of salvation, and the sword of the Spirit, which is the word of God.
—Ephesians 6:17 (ESV)

Finally, be strong in the Lord and in the strength of his might. Put on the whole armor of God, that you may be able to stand against the schemes of the devil.
—Ephesians 6:10–11 (ESV)

Seek Shelter

But you, O Lord, are a shield about me, my glory, and the lifter of my head.
—Psalm 3:3 (ESV)

My shield is with God, who saves the upright in heart.
—Psalm 7:10 (ESV)

The Lord is my rock and my fortress and my deliverer, my God, my rock, in whom I take refuge, my shield, and the horn of my salvation, my stronghold.

—Psalm 18:2 (ESV)

This God—his way is perfect; the word of the Lord proves true; he is a shield for all those who take refuge in him.

—Psalm 18:30 (ESV)

You have given me the shield of your salvation, and your right hand supported me, and your gentleness made me great.

—Psalm 18:35 (ESV)

The Lord is my strength and my shield; in him my heart trusts, and I am helped; my heart exults, and with my song I give thanks to him.

—Psalm 28:7 (ESV)

Our soul waits for the Lord; he is our help and our shield.

—Psalm 33:20 (ESV)

RUN THE RACE

Do you not know that in a race all the runners run, but only one receives the prize? So run that you may obtain it. Every athlete exercises self-control in all things.

—1 Corinthians 9:24–25a (ESV)

Do all things without grumbling or disputing, that you may be blameless and innocent, children of God without blemish in the midst of a crooked and twisted generation, among whom you shine as lights in the world, holding fast to the word of life, so that in the day of Christ I may be proud that I did not run in vain or labor in vain.

—Philippians 2:14–16 (ESV)

Therefore, since we are surrounded by so great a cloud of witnesses, let us also lay aside every weight, and sin which clings so closely, and let us run with endurance the race that is set before us, [2] looking to Jesus, the founder and perfecter of our faith, who for the joy that was set before him endured the cross, despising the shame, and is seated at the right hand of the throne of God.

—Hebrews 12:1–2 (ESV)

With respect to this they are surprised when you do not join them in the same flood of debauchery, and they malign you.

—1 Peter 4:4 (ESV)

I will run in the way of your commandments when you enlarge my heart!

—Psalm 119:32 (ESV)

Come to me, all who labor and are heavy laden, and I will give you rest. Take my yoke upon you, and learn from me, for I am gentle and lowly in heart, and you will find rest for your souls. For my yoke is easy, and my burden is light."

—Matthew 11:28–30 (ESV)

Therefore, if anyone is in Christ, he is a new creation. The old has passed away; behold, the new has come.

—2 Corinthians 5:17 (ESV)

Toolbox Extras

TEMPTATION

For we do not have a high priest who is unable to sympathize with our weaknesses, but one who in every respect has been tempted as we are, yet without sin.

—HEBREWS 4:15 (ESV)

I will meditate on your precepts and fix my eyes on your ways.

—PSALM 119:15 (ESV)

This Book of the Law shall not depart from your mouth, but you shall meditate on it day and night, so that you may be careful to do according to all that is written in it. For then you will make your way prosperous, and then you will have good success.

—JOSHUA 1:8 (ESV)

Practice these things, immerse yourself in them, so that all may see your progress.

—1 TIMOTHY 4:15 (ESV)

PRAYER

Pray then like this: "Our Father in heaven, hallowed be your name. Your kingdom come, your will be done, on earth as it is in heaven. Give us this day our daily bread, and forgive us our debts, as we also have forgiven our debtors. And lead us not into temptation, but deliver us from evil."

—MATTHEW 6:9–13 (ESV)

Do not be anxious about anything, but in everything by prayer and supplication with thanksgiving let your requests be made known to God. And the peace of God, which surpasses all understanding, will guard your hearts and your minds in Christ Jesus.

—Philippians 4:6–7 (ESV)

Printed in the United States
By Bookmasters